# Aaron Burr's Dream
## for the
## Southwest

AARON BURR

# Aaron Burr's Dream
# for the
# Southwest

*A DRAMA FOR THE LIBRARY*

By

Thomas B. Sweeney, Litt. D.

*Published in Connection with the*
*Bi-Centennial Anniversary of the*
*Birth of Aaron Burr on February 6, 1756*

THE NAYLOR COMPANY
San Antonio, Texas

*Other Books by the Author*

HORIZON FRAMES

LEGEND OF LEONARDO

FLIGHT TO ERIN

SUNWARD

MAKERS OF WAR

RHYMES AT ODD TIMES

LIFE UNDERWRITING
   — As a Professional Career

Copyright, 1955

by

THOMAS B. SWEENEY

# Foreword

The story of Aaron Burr has for 150 years been discussed pro and con. While casting about many years ago for a subject which would interest me, Aaron Burr was suggested as the most colorful and controversial character in American history. The more I read about him the more fascinated I became and the more amazed that so many persons seemed to know little about him but to have formed an opinion that he was a scoundrel. On the last page of Dr. Walter Flavius McCaleb's *The Aaron Burr Conspiracy* I found the following:

"The writer stood at the foot of Burr's grave and beside him was Woodrow Wilson, then president of Princeton. With bowed heads we stood for a moment in silence. Suddenly Wilson spoke, his voice pitched very low: 'How misunderstood — how maligned!' Why is it that nearly all the really great souls that come down to us are misunderstood and broken in the gins of life?"

The life of Aaron Burr was filled with drama from the cradle to the grave. He was born February 6, 1756, and was buried at Princeton beside the graves of his father and grandfather, the first and second presidents of Princeton, on September 14, 1836. It would seem that he was frustrated by fate. His sensitive pride and independence of mind prevented him from answering in kind the slanders of Hamilton and Jefferson, his chief opponents.

A student of the times in which he lived cannot refrain from wondering what a difference it might have made to the United States if his advice had been followed at the Battle of Quebec. Would Canada have been part of the United States? What a difference it might have made if Washington had sent him as Minister to France; or if he had been allowed to conquer the Spanish colonies in Mexico and Texas. His chief fault was that he lived forty or fifty years ahead of his age. Like Hamilton and unlike Jefferson, he was an exponent of centralized power. He was responsible for the founding of the Bank of the Manhattan Co. at a time when banks were extremely unpopular. It is interesting to note that this bank and the Chase National have recently merged as the second greatest bank in the world.

I am not attempting to paint Aaron Burr as a superman and certainly not as one depraved. My hope is to produce a portrait of one of the world's most unusual individuals, such as, for example, Leonardo da Vinci. We are all victims of heredity. Genius and insanity are separated by a small margin which changes in degree from age to age. Both were present in Aaron Burr's ancestry.

The following are among the many books upon which this story is based:

*Memoirs of Aaron Burr,* by Matthew L. Davis, 1837

*Life and Times of Aaron Burr,* by J. Parton, 1858

*The Aaron Burr Conspiracy,* by Walter Flavius McCaleb, 1936

*Democracy in America,* by Alexis de Roqueville, 1835

*Aaron Burr, the Proud Pretender,* by Holmes Alexander, 1937

*Jefferson in Power,* by Claude G. Bower, 1936

*Jefferson, the Forgotten Man,* by Samuel B. Pettingill, 1938

*History of the American People,* by Woodrow Wilson, 1901

*George Washington,* by Washington Irving, 1855

*Blennerhassett Island,* by A. F. Gibbons, 1906

*Alexander Hamilton,* by H. T. Ford, 1920

*Alexander Hamilton,* by Lodge, 1899

*Life of John Marshall,* by Alfred Beveridge, 1916

*Washington and His Colleagues,* by Henry Jones Ford, 1918

*Jefferson and His Colleagues,* by Allen Johnson, 1921

*John Marshall and the Constitution,* by Edward S. Gorwin, 1919

— T. B. S.

vii

# Aaron Burr's Dream
# for the
# Southwest

*A Drama for the Library*

By THOMAS B. SWEENEY

## CONTENTS

# Introduction

*The Hon. Henry Fountain Ashurst*

*(Ex-Senator from Arizona)*

Although Aaron Burr's career partook of the nature of a tragedy, Burr was neither theatrical nor artificial. His mental power, splendid military services, fine address, courtesy, courage, pungent intellect, scholarship, descendancy of distinguished families are well-known. The mystery: why, with such advantages, did he fail to hold public esteem?

No politician could have survived the sustained enmity of Washington or the bitter hatred of Jefferson, yet Burr fell out with each of them. To understand why he fell out with them, one must understand not only Burr, but also understand the character, methods and ambitions of the politicians of Burr's day.

The manuscript of Mr. Sweeney's drama evinces diligence and painstaking and wide research. His dialogue is well-sustained — brilliant. I believe that I am eligible to examine an historical work and express an opinion upon the degree of accuracy maintained by the historian; I am also rash enough to venture opinions upon the soundness of the conclusions the historian may draw. I cannot, however, make even a remote approach toward appraising plays. The ability to write tragedy, drama, fiction and fictionized history calls for a special talent — one which would seem to be inborn

xi

and which the author here demonstrates that he possesses.

Such slender, meager talent for appraising plays as I do possess, however, emboldens me to say that this production is interesting and stately in rhetoric, with some events and speeches gorgeously imagined. The author of a play must himself decide what situations he desires his characters to occupy, what words his characters shall speak and what fate shall befall his stage people. Just how far from the facts of history a playwright may choose to depart and what imaginary events and speeches shall be brought upon the stage is for the writer to determine — of this the author is king-emperor. If Mr. Sweeney's drama of Aaron Burr is ever set upon stage or screen, I'll gladly give my last dollar to see it.

# Aaron Burr's Dream for the Southwest

## ACT ONE

### SCENE ONE

SCENE: *Late afternoon of a bright June day in the year 1772. Commencement Day. The Library of Dr. John Witherspoon, President of the College of New Jersey, Princeton.*

*It is a spacious room with two windows opening out on the quiet village street; an oak door to the right; a fireplace and mantel on the left; a handsome chandelier hanging from the center of the ceiling; the walls lined with books except spaces for three large portraits in heavy guilt frames — one of the Reverend Aaron Burr, the first President of the College; one of the latter's wife, Esther Edwards; and one over the mantel of Esther's father, the famous philosopher and Presbyterian minister, Jonathan Edwards, who succeeded his son-in-law, the Reverend Aaron Burr, as President when the latter died.*

1

*A flat-top table occupies the center of the room with heavy arm-chairs, a horse-hair sofa and several foot stools interspersed. A new-fashioned oil lamp, with a large shade, is on one side of the table, and the doctor's quill pen and writing pad and ink, and several books are on the other side. The brass fender reflects the sunlight from the windows. The floor is covered with an Oriental rug. The door into the hall stands open. There is an English clock on the mantel showing the hour as 4 p. m.*

*The sound of a brass knocker is heard from the hall. An English maid appears and admits a man of medium height and middle age, slightly bald and dressed in a well-fitting dark homespun suit.*

TIMOTHY:

I am Timothy Edwards from Elizabethtown.
I came to call on Doctor Witherspoon,
Who said that he would probably be delayed.
I am also expecting my nephew, Aaron Burr,
To meet me. He was graduated today
And I came over for the exercises.

MAID:

Have a seat, sir. Doctor Witherspoon
I'm sure will be here any minute.

[*The maid smilingly retires and Timothy walks over to the portrait of his father and looks at it intently.*]

TIMOTHY:

Yes, that's my father's mouth — his eyes, his hands,
Strong in hurling God's wrath. Those lips condemned
All human beings to the fires of hell
Unless they pled that they were miscreants,
Unworthy in the sight of God to live —
In anguish pled for God to rescue them.
No doubt my father's doctrine was correct.
I've tried in vain to teach it to my nephew.

2

[*Walks a few steps away, then turns back toward the picture.*]

Young Aaron loves the flesh pots of Egypt!
Ignoring me, he only plays a part —
And yet I have a duty to perform.
My father's face now tells me I have failed;
That I am putty in young Aaron's hands.
To conquer him, I flogged him like a sack,
And then he ran away to far New York,
Enlisted as a sailor on a ship.
I tracked him down and found him on that mast.
I should have let him jump into the sea
Instead of promising no punishment
If he returned peacefully to his home.
I lost control I never can regain.
Aaron has the willpower of the devil.

[*With a deep sigh*]

I still shall try to expiate my guilt!
I will be strong and firm like you, father.
I'll try to save him from the fires of hell.

[*Timothy takes out his lace handkerchief and wipes his brow as he walks to the portrait of his sister.*]

Poor Esther, you were much too young to die.
You were the third among my eight sisters —
The prettiest and the best, it seems to me.
What a weird, incongruous lot we were,
With scars of homicidal insanity —
One killed her child; another, his sister;
Two were opium fiends; our aunt an idiot!
Why did you marry that preacher, Aaron Burr,
Aged thirty-seven when you were twenty-one!
Why did you die and leave me guardian
Of Sallie, four, and Aaron, only three!
I think Aaron is incorrigible.

[*Then glancing at the clock he exclaims:*]

3

Already he is fifteen minutes late.

[*He then wanders over to the portrait of Reverend Burr.*]

Why did you ever enter my father's door —
You only complicated all our lives!
Of course, you left the money to support
Your children and pay me as their guardian.
I've done my best; but Aaron is a problem.
His mother called him shy and mischievous,
Requiring a stern governor to control.

[*Two young men suddenly bound into the room from the right — Aaron and his friend Matthias Ogden. They are both handsome, graceful, and about five feet seven inches tall — typical representatives of college boys of their time.*]

AARON:
Sorry to be late, Uncle Timothy.
I saw you in the audience. Thanks for coming.

TIMOTHY:
I felt it was my duty to be here.
Now that you are through college, I have plans
For you to study law. I'll find a tutor.

AARON:
What's that? The law! Perhaps some day, not now.
I am staying here at Princeton for a while
To do some post-graduate work. It's all arranged!
I'll have full access to the library.
Yes, I've talked it over with Doctor Witherspoon.
I brought Matt along. As you know, we're classmates.

[*The Young man shakes hands with Timothy, who turns to Aaron.*]

TIMOTHY:
I think it time for you to settle down.
I understand you partially frittered away
Your senior year, and spent your time in play.

4

OGDEN [*With astonishment*]:
  Mister Edwards, how can you say that,
  When Aaron led his class with highest honors —
  A *Summa Cum Laude* — and he just sixteen!
  He didn't have to work. He just absorbs
  A page and then remembers what is on it.

TIMOTHY:
  So that's it! A genius now, you say!
  I'll talk it over myself with Doctor Witherspoon.
  I know I have a duty to perform.

  [*The sound of horses hoofs is heard on the cobble pavement. The boys dash to the open window and lean out.*]

AARON:
  All right, Corinne, we are coming down at once.
  Goodbye, Uncle Timothy, we shall come back later.
  I shall write you all my plans quite soon.
  Please don't worry about me. I'll promise to make good.
  Give my love to Aunt Esther. I'll see her soon.

  [*Ogden disappears through the door.*]

TIMOTHY [*Quite perturbed*]:
  Wait, Aaron, I want to caution you once more!
  Your tendency to go to such extremes
  Is caused by the insanity which runs
  In my family, and which is in your blood.

AARON:
  Well, Uncle Timothy, I'll say again;
  If I have inherited insanity
  There is nothing I can do about it.
  I am what I am and will so remain.

  [*Aaron dashes out of the room. The boys' voices are heard as they talk to the two girls in the cut-under and the beat of the horses' hoofs is again heard. Timothy looks out of the window and sighs. He*

5

*mops his brow and paces the room. Doctor Wither-
spoon enters from the left and cordially shakes hands
with Timothy. He is a tall, kindly-looking man, in
powdered wig, neatly fitting breeches and long coat,
with light-colored waistcoat and high stock.*]

WITHERSPOON:
I am sorry to have kept you waiting.

TIMOTHY:
I have been very painfully occupied,
Examining my soul beneath these frames.

[*Waving his hand toward the portraits*]

WITHERSPOON:
Your nephew is the youngest in his class.
He has carried off the highest honors.
I congratulate you on his success.
We have had a number of serious talks
About the nature of the Deity.
He is quite precocious and I like him.
I have consented to let him stay on here
A while with access to the library,
Until he can determine on his future —
That is, of course, with your complete concurrence.

TIMOTHY:
Very well, I do concur, but I shall hope
For word from you if he gets into mischief,
As he is only sixteen and my ward.

WITHERSPOON:
Now that is settled. We shall keep in touch.
What a pity his father died so soon —
But he lived long enough to build Nassau Hall!
I am deeply interested in his son,
Despite his flippant ideas about God,
Despite his wasted nights in those taverns!

TIMOTHY:
I was afraid of that! I can do nothing.

6

WITHERSPOON:
I shall try to put God into his heart!
Those hours in the library will not help.
He has inherited a strong will power.
His ambition to excel is amazing.
He studies sixteen hours a day or more!
He can read Latin and Greek fluently.
Perhaps God has some worthy objective —
At any rate, I'll see what I can do!
I owe it to his father's memory.
I shall urge more religious reading,
And less of those godless French philosophers.

TIMOTHY [*Rising and extending his hand*]:
Aaron is fortunate to have a friend like you.
Tell him I'm sorry that he had to leave.

[*Timothy bows and leaves the room.*]

WITHERSPOON [*Walking toward the shelf to select a book and looking at the portrait above*]:

What a remarkable family they are!
Those brilliant black eyes of the grandfather,
Piercing and filled with fanaticism,
Burn in the orbs of Timothy and Aaron.

[*A loud knock is heard, followed by the entrance of Aaron Burr.*]

AARON:
Excuse me, Doctor Witherspoon, I thought
That Uncle Timothy would still be here.

WITHERSPOON:
He just now left. He wants to shape your life.

AARON:
I do not want him thinking that I am rude,
But I shall shape my life without his help.
I know that I must have a life's vocation.
I want to study law, but first, stay here
And profit by this wonderful library.

7

WITHERSPOON:
>    That is agreed. Your uncle fully concurs.
>    May I suggest that you extend your reading
>    To include your grandfather's great work,
>    "New Life Philosophy"! One of your classmates,
>    Young Breckenridge, has written a fine thesis,
>    "The Rising Glory of America."
>    A young man's feet must be upon the ground!
>    I fear your ideas soar among the clouds!

AARON:
>    That is exactly why I am staying here.
>    I want to get my feet upon the ground.

WITHERSPOON:
>    My ancestor, John Knox, had followers
>    Whose works are worth exploring while you're here —
>    That is, if you're ambitious to improve
>    And broaden all the viewpoints of your life.

AARON:
>    But I am not going into the ministry.
>    In fact, I am not sure there is a God —
>    I mean a personal God who counts one's hairs
>    And cares more for a man than for a beast!
>    I know there is order in the universe —
>    Who dares deny it with the setting sun,
>    The constant rise and fall of ocean tides,
>    The phases of the moon — the Spring and Fall!
>    There is a God, impossible to know!
>    A fly knows I am here — but that is all!
>    Just so, a man has knowledge of a God!

WITHERSPOON:
>    I shall not let you talk that way of God!
>    But I respect your confidence, of course.
>    I cannot recommend the ministry,
>    But you are a child of God. He has given you
>    Unusual gifts of mind to do His work
>    And benefit mankind. I caution you
>    To use those gifts as God would have you do.

8

AARON:

> Doctor Witherspoon, we do not look alike
> On life or God and yet we both aspire
> To follow what is good and shun the evil.
> You are subservient to your God's will.
> I am independent, and yet I serve the good!
> We know we have a span to live, then die.
> You will spend that span preparing for Heaven.
> I shall spend it to promote my interests here —
> Not knowing a thing about elusive Heaven!
> We'll both be honest with ourselves and God!
> Strangely enough, we worship the same God
> But how differently do we regard Him!
> You think He can be analyzed! I don't!

WITHERSPOON:

> Aaron, my son, I can't permit such talk —
> Yet I respect your deep integrity
> And pray for your eventual conversion
> To the teaching of the great John Knox!
> Meantime, please freely use the library
> And come to me for frequent consultations.

AARON:

> I am grateful for this opportunity.
> I promise not to bring disgrace on you,
> But ask your indulgence if I should offend.
> I must be just myself and carry on
> As nature and heredity dictate.
> I honor my grandfather and my father
> As men of invincible character.
> But for myself, I was born a free-lance.
> I think for myself without restriction.

WITHERSPOON:

> You are too young to be so self-confident.
> I must implore you to change your attitude
> Toward God. Just put yourself into His hands.
> Your soul's salvation rests upon your faith.

9

AARON:

I shall consider all that you have said.
I'll try to find the truth, also the light,
But I fear it will not be my grandfather's
"New Light." Instead I'll try to find my own!
I'll gladly come to you for sympathy,
If you will so permit, but not advice!
I must decide my course in life alone.
Instead of sacred books, for the time being
I'm reading the exploits of Emperor Frederick.
I admire the military profession.

WITHERSPOON [*Looking at the small hands and delicate features of his pupil*]:

Aaron, I think I did the proper thing
To refuse to let you enter Princeton
At the age of eleven, even though you could
Read Virgil and the Grecian alphabet.
I made you wait two years and then enter Princeton
As a Sophomore, not as a Junior.

AARON:

Doctor Witherspoon, of course I've known all this.

WITHERSPOON:

Aaron, I think you're better fitted by nature
For a literary occupation
Than for a military career.
Take your time, my son, and God will guide you.
Your essays have shown eloquence and feeling —
For instance, "Origin of Idolatry."
I think you are a literary man.

[*Just here, another knocking at the hall door is heard.*]

AARON [*Rising and smiling*]:

I must be going. I shall remember
All that you have said and profit by it.

10

WITHERSPOON [*Also rising*]:
   That is the faculty for consultation.
   Wait here till I return. I will tell them
   About your freedom to use the library.

   [*He leaves the room and closes the door*]

AARON [*Looking after him and pacing the floor*]:
   What do these stupid mortals think I am —
   A lump of clay to fashion into molds;
   A child, or dog to lead upon a leash!
   I'll show them all that I am now a man.
   No living person now, or ever shall
   Control my thinking, or a single move.
   I'm here upon this earth to play a part.
   I am not an imbecile! I'm not a child!
   Could anyone direct my father's will?
   Old Jonathan himself once rocked the earth!
   Heredity has made me what I am!
   I'll hew my path, make progerss step by step.
   No man can ever break me to his will!
   My star will shine! The world will know my name!
   Just how or by what means, I shall decide!

   [*Doctor Witherspoon returns with the faculty, Aaron
   bowing gracefully to each.*]

A FACULTY MEMBER [*Looking intently at Aaron and
   shaking his hand*]:

   Aaron, as you know, I am librarian
   I shall assist you to take advantage
   Of this unusual opportunity.

WITHERSPOON:
   We shall all help you. Come to me often.

AARON:
   Thank you sir. I shall gladly do so.

   [*As the faculty members take their seats, talking
   among themselves, Aaron leaves the room.*]

                                              CURTAIN

                                                   11

# ACT ONE

## SCENE TWO

SCENE: *Richmond Hill. A brilliant sun lights up the spacious private office of George Washington at Richmond Hill, the large colonial manor house in New York, which has been rented as his headquarters since Bunker Hill. It is a splendor of white columns and gardened lawns, sloping down to the Hudson at the corner of Charlton and Varick Streets. Six years have elapsed. It is the fall of 1778. Aaron Burr, now 22, is closely examining the map of Quebec — one of the many large maps which line the walls. He is taller and broader, and his face and figure very handsome in his uniform of a Lieutenant Colonel of the United States Army. He looks very mature as a grown man, but his face shows a strain and his nervous manner is that of an ill person. He walks up and down the room glancing at the gorgeous view through the windows, frequently stopping at the maps of Quebec and Princeton, but his eyes keep turning to the heavy oak door of the room. He is evidently waiting for someone to enter. Finally his thin body sags wearily into a large oak chair, his head sinks forward, his eyes stare sadly at nothing.*

AARON:
It all comes back as though but yesterday.
Poor Witherspoon's concern for my lost soul!
Those last six months in Princeton's library —
And then at Doctor Bellamy's foul school
Which taught me to despise man's narrow creeds.
I hold the road to heaven is open to all!
Those village girls alone preserved my life.
My only happiness was their embrace!
And then came Lexington and Bunker Hill!
I seized the chance, enlisted in the cause —
For glory, and to save the colonies.

12

[*He jumps up nervously and goes to the window,
glances about and returns listlessly to his chair.*]

Then George Washington from Virginia came to
    rule —
A stupid man who cannot punctuate
Or spell, but deals in ponderous sentences!
I was his secretary, so I should know!
Why should a man like that out-rank Pomeroy,
Artemus Ward, John Hancock, or Charlie Lee!
I'm glad that I learned Emperor Frederick's art —
When to retreat and when to attack and win!
Benedict Arnold's plan to take Quebec
Would have succeeded, had they listened to me.

[*He sighs deeply.*]

Twelve hundred of us dared those rugged wilds —
Four hundred miles from Fort Western to Quebec,
Through snow, torrential rains and frozen mud —
Huge green-pine batteaux carried through the mire
And over fallen logs, up sky-steep slopes!
Three hundred men succumbed; but I escaped!

[*He goes to the map of Canada on the wall, showing
mountains and streams. He smiles broadly.*]

Dear Jacataqua, half-caste Indian maid!
You warmed me, fed me bear meat, saved my life!
Where are you now? Where is our little child?
My dearest friend, Matt Ogden, classmate, chum,
You and I explored the frozen paths!
How we survived, the God of Heaven knows!
A dreadful hurricane raged through the woods —
A mighty giant felling all the trees
Within its path — then the captain's boat —
I at the prow — plunged down the rapids' falls!
With one man killed, but you and I were spared!
How have I lived to reach this bitter hour!

[*Then glancing again at the map showing Quebec.*]

Colonel Arnold had secured a scanty store
To provision what was left — five hundred men —
Five hundred bearded skeletons in rags.
He had conceived the very doubtful plan
Of joining with Montgomery, then flushed
With victories at Saint John's and Montreal.
To find him was the point! Where could he be?
Disguised as a youthful priest he sent me out.
A monastery furnished me a guide —
My French and Latin patois was the bait —
And soon General Montgomery and I were friends.
He commissioned me a captain on his staff —
This just reward I felt was fully due!

[*He shows much emotion.*]

And then we faced Quebec — my greatest thrill!
To scale Cape Diamond bastion, I said —
With feigned attacks along the outer walls —
Would bring success! The council chose my plan!
My fifty men, upon a snowy night,
Would scale the wall and turn the batteries
Upon surprised defenders, open gates
Through which our boys would rush. It could not
    fail!
If we succeeded, Canada would be ours!
But no snow came! Montgomery could not wait.
He changed my plan. The Lower Town he'd seize,
And after that the fort upon the crest!

[*Becoming more excited, walking back and forth,
with his hands to his head.*]

I see right now those lines of picket fence;
I hear the blast of guns above the storm;
We knew a block-house fortified the lane —
And yet we saw no sentries — all was still.
I heard the general say, "Quebec is ours!"
I pled with him in vain to stay behind!
And then concealed twelve-pounders flung their
    charge!

14

The narrow lane was clogged with dying men —
All who had entered, killed except myself —
All victims of that ill-advised assault!
The general lay within a pool of blood.
I waved my sword and shouted to advance,
But all were cowards. Not one obeyed my call.
We could have conquered if just one hundred men
Had come at once! It was our only chance!
How I escaped, I will never know!
I dragged Montgomery's body to the rear,
And then collapsed! Defeat, not victory —
And all because he would not take my advice!

[*He flings himself, limp, into the chair, as a loud
knock is heard, and Matthias Ogden enters the room.
He is in his Colonel's uniform, his eyes sparkling,
his arms extended. Aaron rises and embraces him,
but shows that he is about to faint.*]

OGDEN:
For God's sake, Aaron, what's the matter with you?
You look like a ghost. Where is Washington?

AARON:
I'm a sick man. I'm waiting for the General
To hand him my resignation, right now!
I've been sitting here thinking of my fate.
These maps have brought back many memories.
I've been living over my wasted years.
This is no reflection on you, my friend.
I know it was entirely due to you
That I was placed on General Washington's staff,
Even if only a secretary.
He ignores my advice, and I am through!

OGDEN:
You are not through! You are only discouraged.
No man of your brief years has ever before
Received so much applause when all the world
Learned of your feat of carrying and dragging
The heavy corpse of General Montgomery

15

Alone and unassisted to the rear —
With bullets all around! Yet you escaped!
But only by the grace of God, all say!

AARON:
    I will admit it was my life's high point!
    But only look at what has happened since.

OGDEN:
    Well, tell me what it is that's happened since!
    Your advancement in the ranks has been unique.
    Lieutenant Colonel, at only twenty-two!
    I have not seen you for a year — and yet
    Your letters have been cheerful. Tell me all.

[*They both take chairs and Aaron continues his narrative.*]

AARON:
    I know that Canada was lost by chance.
    I could have won it, but they would not hear —
    My present to the Colonies disdained!
    I knew that Arnold was our George's pet.
    I knew that he could not be trusted far —
    A coward! I resolved to leave his staff.
    Confronting General Arnold, I resigned,
    Defying him to stop me in my flight.

OGDEN:
    That is where you made your first mistake.
    You should have stayed till Canada was taken.

AARON [*Ignoring the interruption*]:
    In coming South I met democracy —
    A chimera of stupid, foolish brains.
    The animal called man, like all the rest,
    Must have a leader. Such is the law of life.
    In the Hudson Valley and Connecticut,
    I saw the crops destroyed, men hanged, homes
        burned —
    All in the name of fancied liberty!

16

OGDEN:
Well, what did you expect? War makes men beasts!

AARON [*Waving his hand toward the scenery showing through the windows*]:

And then New York! This Richmond Hill I love.
The British fleet, with thirty thousand troops,
I found was anchored off the Battery.
I urged our General to burn the town,
Not fight the British hordes. "A beardless boy,"
He called me! But John Hancock was my friend!
As President of Congress, we conspired.
He had me transferred to a new command.
George Washington and I could not agree.
As General Putnam's aide I was content —
Especially as his house guest, Mag Moncrieffe,
Became my paramour at age fourteen.
To me she claimed she "plighted virgin vows!"
Seduction is no crime if met halfway.

OGDEN:
Aaron, I have always said women would ruin you.

AARON:
George Washington had built two puny forts.
The British came in rowboats up the river.
I begged that we unite in one defense.
Not so! Both forts were seized in record time.
Ten thousand Hessian mercenaries came
And chased our patriots across the land!
Had my advice been followed, we should have won!
But no, a "beardless boy" must not prevail!

OGDEN:
I can see your rage. What did you do then?

AARON:
Then back to Princeton with poor Putnam's troops!
I won each skirmish when I was in charge.
George Washington then crossed the Delaware
At Trenton, captured those weak Hessian troops,

17

And then, by ambuscade at Princeton, caught
The British in his subtly-baited trap.
The tide was turned by Washington, not me!
I would have saved ten thousand valued lives,
Not counting wasted time and countless stores!

OGDEN [*Who can stand this tirade no longer, jumps up
and shakes Aaron by the shoulder*]:

Wake up, Aaron. You are indeed a sick man.

[*He goes to the cupboard in the wall and brings a
decanter of grog, a glass and a pitcher of water, pours
out a diluted quantity of grog and forces Aaron to
drink it, although the latter shows his distate for it.*]

That will help you. You have been doing too much.
I heard of how you drilled those new recruits
From early morning until late at night;
How you made them efficient soldiers;
How you have not spared yourself, day or night!
Now you must have a rest — a real change.
You are too useful to be neglected.

AARON:

Yes, that is it! I want to be useful —
But in some other field, not in the army!

[*He has visibly recovered himself and has come out
of his fit of depression.*]

That is why I'm here. I must have a change.
Law, my early ambition — with no boss
To interfere and thwart my well-laid plans!
George Washington cannot endure having a man
Around him of an independent mind.
Ask Captain Alexander Hamilton what he thinks.
I heard him say, "He is a Southern Planter,
A poor general; an honest but weak man."

OGDEN:

Hamilton! Is not that the artillery captain

18

Who had lost his baggage and lost his way,
And was being chased back to Harlem
By the Red Coats, when you and two horsemen
Ran across them as you were riding home?

AARON:
That is correct — and what fun we had!

OGDEN:
Didn't you turn them back by intrepid orders
And chase them to their ships, taking prisoners?

AARON [*Becoming excited, rising and pacing the floor*]:
Yes, I can see them running like scared rabbits.
It was for that exploit that I received
My commission as Lieutenant Colonel —
Brought to me by others, not Washington!

OGDEN:
It seems that you and he cannot get along.

AARON:
General Putnam gave me a free rein.
I was in sole command of his regiment.
You know what I did in Orange County!
Despite the General's orders to retreat,
I fell upon the enemy at night
And forced two thousand of them to retreat,
With fearful loss, leaving behind the cattle
They had stolen, and all their ammunition!
Next day Washington ordered my regiment
To join the main body at Philadelphia,
Where he was fighting the British hand to hand.
Thus my exploit was completely nullified.
You see my hands were tied then as now!

[*He takes a seat and looks at Ogden for a reply.*]

OGDEN:
It seems you can't stand being under orders.
For that reason, I must agree with you
That the army is not the place for you.
You must be free to act independently.

19

AARON:

Thanks, Matt! You understand me, but few do.
There is one other who gives me confidence
By her sympathy and understanding.
I'm lifted out of my gloom in her presence.

OGDEN:

I've heard rumors that you rescued three ladies
From a rioting mob at Paramus,
And that since then you visit them frequently.

AARON:

You're right. Mrs. Prevost facinates me.
She and her sister are highly cultured.
She is a widow and has five children.
Her English husband, Colonel Prevost, was killed
Fighting in the West Indies, a year ago.

OGDEN:

Don't look so serious, Aaron, I know you
And your fascination for women,
But they are always young things that claim you.

AARON:

The Hermitage, their home at Paramus,
Is the rendezvous of all our officers
And their wives — including the Washingtons.
I must take you there! Oh, what a library!

[*At this moment, George Washington enters the
room. Colonel Burr and Colonel Ogden, taken by
surprise, rise and bow. Washington's tall figure, brilliant
uniform and epaulets overshadow the two
young officers. He is now forty-six. He bows in return
and sits down wearily in his chair by his desk
and gives each of his young officers a searching
glance.*]

WASHINGTON:

Gentlemen, be seated. Sorry to be late.
Colonel Burr, you have been waiting some time.

20

AARON:

> General Washington, I must tell you frankly
> I want to retire from the service —
> If you will be so kind as to permit it.
> I have consulted several doctors,
> And it's upon their advice I am acting.
> My nervous condition is such, I can't sleep.
> Since that night I slept exhausted on damp ground,
> After chasing the Hessians to their ships,
> A gnawing fever is sapping my strength.
> I have brought you this written request
> Asking for release from duty without pay.

> [*He hands General Washington the letter, which
> Washington rapidly scans.*]

WASHINGTON:

> You carry your idea of delicacy too far,
> Colonel Burr; of course you will draw your pay.
> I'll assign you to a less arduous post.
> In fact I've anticipated your request,
> And have discussed it all with our good friend,
> Mrs. Prevost. I've decided to place you
> In command at West Point. Your duty will be
> To protect the people of these soverign states
> By keeping all supplies from our enemies.

AARON [*Looking despairingly at Ogden*]:

> I thank you, sir. I shall do my best.

WASHINGTON:

> Now that that is settled, may I say
> Mrs. Washington and I expect you both
> To dine with us. It will be no novelty
> For Colonel Burr. For several exciting months
> This was his home. He must feel at ease here.

AARON:

> Richmond Hill is my ideal of a home.

> [*Three ladies enter the room, all dressed in the styles
> of the day — Mrs. Washington, now forty-three, very*

21

*chic and smiling, talking vivaciously to her friend,*
*Mrs. Prevost, and the latter's sister, Miss de Visme.*
*The young men rise and bow to the ladies, then*
*bring up chairs surrounding General Washington.*]

WASHINGTON:
This has been a most exciting day.
The Marquis Lafayette has reported
That Louis has promised Marie Antoinette
That, since we won at Saratoga,
He will recognize us as a nation.
That Benjamin Franklin, by his astute ways
And benevolent manner, has won the Queen
And all her followers to our country's cause!
To at last be recognized by France
Assures our independence without a doubt!

[*An orderly enters the room and announces dinner.*
*They all rise and their chatter is blended in an in-*
*articulate sound of words as they walk slowly toward*
*the door. Aaron walks by the side of Mrs. Prevost and*
*they are talking in whispers and looking into each*
*other's eyes.*]

WASHINGTON [*Standing by his desk alone*]:
A conceited young bounder, but very brave;
A fearless leader under heavy fire;
And yet I cannot trust him to obey!
He jeopardized our troops at Hackensack
Because he thought his was a better plan!
He put down that rebellion at Valley Forge;
With his own sword, cut off a rebel's arm
Who raised his gun and shouted to the men
To seize their youthful Colonel then and there.
A less intrepid leader would have failed —
God only knows what might have happened then!
And yet I shall be glad to send him off.
Insubordination in the heart
Of any officer puts all at risk,
Even though his talents be superb!

22

At West Point he can recuperate, I hope,
And be less tempted to upset my plans.

[*As he leaves the room, through the door on left,
Aaron dashes in and picks up Mrs. Prevost's Persian
shawl which she had left on her chair. He drapes
it on his arm and with excitement and chagrin, mutters to himself.*]

AARON:
So I must still remain — obedient slave
To this most pompous, stupid General!
Although he is the world's most talked-of man
Since he by chance defeated old Burgoyne!
If he takes my advice, this war will cease.
He's but a child compared to Frederick!
Why can't he see I'm right? I'd rather die
Than be subservient to such a man!

[*He hastens from the room with the shawl on his
arm.*]

CURTAIN

# ACT ONE

## SCENE THREE

SCENE:  *The spacious law office of Judge William
Patterson in the village of Raritan in New Jersey,
twenty miles from Brunswick and twenty miles from
Paramus. Two years have passed. It is now the autumn of 1780. Aaron, in civilian clothes, is seated at
a desk in one corner of a room, near a window,
through which the rich autumn coloring of the trees
is seen. The walls are lined with law books and several are piled on his desk. He has a pad and a quill*

23

*pen, and keeps turning from a book to the pad, mak-*
*ing notes on the latter, with a serious expression. His*
*long black hair is tied with a black cord at the nape*
*of his neck, below which it turns up in several tightly-*
*bound loops. He is very earnest in his study and does*
*not hear the closing and latching of the door as Judge*
*Patterson enters and approaches his desk.*

PATTERSON:
Good morning, Aaron. Let me see your notes.

[*He glances at them and then at Aaron.*]

Eighteen hours a day is much too long
For you or anyone to give to study.
I want you, as my pupil, to succeed,
But never at the cost of your good health.
Three years have been prescribed to qualify
For a degree in law. Why kill yourself?

AARON [*Rising and looking squarely at the Judge*]:
Judge Patterson, you know I have ambition.
I have much work to do. I get absorbed
And lose all thought of time. You know I've read
A number of these books at Princeton.

PATTERSON [*Having taken a seat at his desk and study-
ing Aaron's pad*]:

How did you happen to explore this theme?
It is quite excellent, but you must curb
Ambition — or, at least, be reasonable!
In one month you have proved ability
To interpret with intelligence the laws —
No matter how vexatious and intricate.
I am proud of this — but you must take three years!

AARON:
Well, we shall see! Of course, you may be right.
I value your instructions! But as for time
Let circumstances be the judge of that!
Doctor Witherspoon held me back two years.

24

He feared that I was working much too hard.
I ask you to forget the time prescribed
And let my fitness and accomplishments
Decide when I am ready for the bar.

PATTERSON [*Turning again to the pad*]:
Aaron, you are the strangest character I know.
You've inherited the Edwards strong will power,
But I can't sit content and let you break
All precedents, and qualify too soon.

AARON:
Please let the matter rest! Decide it later!

PATTERSON [*Having carefully read Aaron's notes*]:
Aaron, I have marked one sentence to revise.
I think your interpretation of Blackstone wrong.
The other pages seem to be correct.

[*He hands Aaron his pad and leaves the room, as Aaron bows his thanks.*]

[*A knock is heard. Aaron opens the door. Theodosia Prevost enters. She looks ten years older than Aaron, but has a radiant beauty and her face is smiling. Aaron shows surprise and pleasure. They kiss impulsively and walk to Aaron's desk. Theodosia is dressed in a becoming blue brocade gown and a small blue velvet hat. She is very vivacious.*]

THEODOSIA:
Catherine and I drove over from Paramus.
I came right in while she is hitching the horses.

AARON:
I am glad you came. I've been planning my course.
Sit down and let me tell you about it.

[*She takes a chair, Aaron looking into her eyes lovingly.*]

Theodosia, you captured me at once —
Your voice, your face, your eyes, your conversation!

25

You have taught me self-respect and confidence.
You said you would not marry for love alone.
I will pay your price! You are the "governor"
Which my mother always said I needed
As a balance-wheel! My health is restored!
My ambition to succeed and all my hope
For perfect happiness are due to you.
You think I possess the elements of worth!
Yes, for you I shall strive and shall succeed!
They say it takes three years of tutoring
For the law. I shall do it in six months!
In six months I shall claim you as my bride!

[*Catherine enters the room and Aaron kisses her hand.*]

CATHERINE:
I couldn't keep her from coming. She's obsessed!

AARON:
Nothing could please me more than this delightful call.
I have come to a conclusion — a fixed goal!

THEODOSIA:
But wait, Aaron, Judge Patterson tells me
You are killing yourself by too much work.
Your health must be considered. We must wait.

AARON:
What nonsense! Do I look ill or anaemic?
No, I shall prove that I am not just average!
In six months I shall go to Albany
And force the Court to admit me to practice!
I shall pass all tests! They'll make an exception
On account of the time I gave my country.
Then we shall be married and life will begin!

THEODOSIA:
Aaron, we must not be foolish. Health comes first!
Is it true you work eighteen hours each day?

26

AARON:
Now let me attend to that in my own way.
How are those dear children, Frederick and Bartow?

THEODOSIA:
They wanted to come with us. They adore you.

AARON:
I adore them, also their angel mother!

[*He rushes over and kisses her.*]

Tell them I'll have them tutored in law next year.

THEODOSIA:
Aaron, my darling, Catherine has news for you!

CATHERINE:
I'm engaged to Joseph Brown and Mother says,
We must have a double wedding next Spring,
With a reception at the Hermitage.
She feels so sure that your plan will succeed!

AARON:
Bless your dear mother. She can depend on me.
Catherine, I've been expecting this for some time.
I'm fond of Joe and know you will be happy.

[*He rises and pulls the bell cord.*]

It's tea time for Judge and Mrs. Patterson.

[*A colored maid enters the room.*]

Amada, we shall have two friends for tea.

[*The maid bows and leaves the room.*]

AARON [*Turning to his visitors*]:
Please say nothing to them about our wedding.
Judge Patterson expects me to take three years
To prepare for law. Just leave it all to me!
I shall prove to him what I can do.
Excuse me, please, one minute. I'll announce you.

[*He leaves the room.*]

27

THEODOSIA [*Turning to her sister*]:
What can I do or say to such a man!
He certainly is a law unto himself.
The way he now devours Voltaire and Rousseau
And even William Godwin, is amazing.

CATHERINE:
Aaron is not a bit like anyone else.

THEODOSIA [*With despair*]:
The way he drives himself beyond control
Of law and order in this staid old world,
Both frightens me and consecrates my love.
I am convinced that he is a super-man!
What woman would not be proud to be his wife!
No one can resist his fascination.
Even General Washington succumbs, they say.
He looks to me for guidance — we are one!

[*Judge and Mrs. Patterson and Aaron enter the
room, followed by the colored maid with tea and bis-
cuits on a tray. The Pattersons shake hands with their
guests.*]

PATTERSON:
We are always honored to have you call!

MRS. PATTERSON [*As they all take seats*]:
Tell us the latest news about Washington.
Isn't it exciting the way Cornwallis
Is retreating? We have him on the run!
Is it true that Mrs. Benedict Arnold
Told you her part in that tragic event?

THEODOSIA:
It is all quite simple. Yes, she was my friend,
The daughter of Chief Justice Shippen
Of Philadelphia. General Washington
Gave her a passport to join her husband,
General Arnold, in New York City.
She stopped at the Hermitage overnight.
Before leaving West Point, however, she learned

28

That Major Andre of the British army,
With whom she had been corresponding,
Had been captured and her letters were found.
As you know, this led to the charge of treason
Against General Arnold. She was in a state
Of hysterics when she told me her part.
She was hardly able to travel, in fact.
She said it was her fault that the General,
Her husband, was brought into an arrangement
To surrender West Point to the British.

PATTERSON:

It is indeed a very tragic story!
Benedict Arnold will now go down the ages
As another Judas Iscariot,
After all his brilliant work for our cause!

AARON:

I've known that Arnold was untrustworthy!
It was his influence on Montgomery
That lost Quebec. I pleaded with him in vain
To wait for snow, and then to scale the wall
When no one would think we dared! The snow came!
But it was three days too late! We lost Quebec!
Some people call it fate that shapes our lives!
Predestination was my father's faith.
Who knows what it is — heredity or God?
I hold we cannot help being what we are!
Mrs. Arnold, Theodosia's friend,
Was just a blinded link to bring about
The judgment that we now inflict on Arnold!
He deserves the blame for losing Canada
As a vital part of our United States —
But it happened at Quebec, not West Point!

THEODOSIA:

Aaron, please don't be such a fatalist.

AARON:

Anyway, I'm glad I'm out of the army!
Washington and Lafayette are imprinting

29

Their names in history in their different ways.
I mean to imprint mine also, in due time,
But under a different classification!
Those four years in the army taught me life.
I am an ardent admirer of Frederick.
His campaigns taught me that war is cruel,
Cold-blooded, a battle of wits with no quarter!
Then I learned that lesson in my own way!
I learned that our so-called patriots are beasts!

PATTERSON [*Showing surprise*]:
What do you mean, Aaron? You greatly surprise me!

AARON:
The first night I was in command at White Plains
We sent out a party of one hundred men,
Ordered to gather facts about the foe.
Instead, they came back with the spoils they
    plundered
From the farmers living near — bedding, clothing!
Their horses laden down with household goods
Of patriots, not Tories! Their leaders
I consider beasts, deserving to be hanged!

[*Turning to Theodosia.*]

Those months in your library, Theodosia,
Gave me higher concepts of humanity.
Now Chesterfield, to whom you introduced me,
Is my model! Yes, I owe it all to you.

THEODOSIA [*Blushing*]:
No, you do not owe it to me, Aaron,
But to your ambition and your self-respect.

PATTERSON:
I am glad that Aaron is out of the army.
He was killing himself by overwork.
I must persuade him to take life easier,
Now that he has been cured of his ailments.
But he is back again at his old habits

30

Of eighteen hours or more of study daily!
No man can stand that punishment for long.

THEODOSIA [*Looking alarmed*]:
   That is just what I, too, keep on telling him.
   Between us, we may yet save him from himself.

AARON [*Smiling*]:
   I promise that when I feel too much strain,
   I shall relax, and run to your library.

MRS. PATTERSON [*Putting down her teacup*]:
   William, all this has been very pleasant,
   But we must go now and leave our young friends
   To discuss their personal problems alone.
   Do come again soon. You are always welcome.

[*They all rise and Judge and Mrs. Patterson leave the room.*]

AARON [*Turning to Theodosia*]:
   In four months I shall leave Raritan,
   Then stay two important months at Haverstraw
   With my old friend, Thomas Smith, who will teach me
   All the tricks of a legal practitioner!
   Then to Albany, where my devoted friends,
   Generals MacDougall, Schuyler and Clinton,
   Under all of whom I've served with honor,
   Will bring great pressure on Chief Justice Morris
   To admit me to the Bar next Spring!
   Meantime, your letters, Theodosia,
   Will sustain me more than any medicine —
   And, of course, we shall visit back and forth.

THEODOSIA:
   I shall never feel at ease until I can
   Look after you personally, in my own way.
   Meantime, I'll trust you to be prudent
   And not kill yourself by overwork.
   That was my chief reason for coming today!
   I wanted to know how Judge Patterson felt.

AARON:

I am glad you came. Write at least once a week,
But no more coddling or mineral waters!
If only you could sit by and stroke my head
With your little hand, all would be well.

CATHERINE:

I hear that Washington is advancing South,
Leaving New York entirely to the British.
Do you think we are safe, living so near?

AARON:

Perfectly safe. They dare not leave New York
Where they are well protected by their ships.

THEODOSIA:

Aaron, write often. Your letters are precious.
I read them dozens of times and keep them
Under my pillow. Our love is eternal!
We make the world for each other, my darling,

[*Looking at the clock.*]

Now we must go, to reach home before dark.
This will prove a memorable visit for me.

[*Aaron escorts them out of the room, all talking with
friendly intimacy.*]

CURTAIN

# ACT ONE

## SCENE FOUR

SCENE:   *The Hermitage. The rising curtain displays
the large living room of this famous old manor house
which has long been the home of the de Visme family
at Paramus, New Jersey.*

*It is noon of July second, 1782. The sun is shining and through the windows are seen extensive views of the surrounding hills and trees. The room is filled to capacity with men and women all standing in silence and facing the bay window where a black-robed clergyman with an open Bible in his left hand is looking into the eyes of the new bride and groom, Theodosia and Aaron. He is the Reverend David Bogart of the Dutch Reformed Church. He raises his right hand, saying, "I pronounce you man and wife."*

*Aaron is wearing his old every day coat and Theodosia is dressed in her new white gauze wedding gown. They clasp hands and their lips unite in a fervent kiss. Next to them are the tall and handsome Joseph Brown and Catherine, sister of Theodosia, who were the first to be united in this double wedding. They are joined by Mrs. de Visme, mother of the brides, a very dignified English lady of the old school, and her five grandchildren, three tall girls in their teens and the younger boys, Bartow and Frederick, all looking at their mother and Aaron with love in their eyes.*

*The guests pass along in single file, exchanging friendly wishes, some kissing the brides and grooms. The confused blending of sounds makes it impossible to distinguish any conversation. The guests finally depart after making their adieus, leaving only the relatives of the family and a few intimate friends of Aaron and Theodosia.*

*As the room becomes cleared, colored slaves bring in chairs and small tables and place them around the room. The chandelier sheds sparkling rays of light. The ancestral portraits on the walls look down with dignity. The book cases of classic literature become more impressive. The guests who have been asked to remain, now seat themselves at the tables. Wine is served, plates of fruit and food are placed on the*

33

*tables. Reverend Bogart, Mrs. de Visme and Judge Patterson occupy one table; the brides and grooms another; and the Hamiltons and Ogdens still another. The five children are seated at a table alone.*

JUDGE PATTERSON [*Rising, rapping for silence and raising his glass*]:

I know you all will want to drink a toast
To the mother of these very lovely brides
And wish our four young friends much happiness.

[*They all rise and drain their glasses.*]

AARON [*Rising*]:
My brother-in-law has asked me to thank
Our mother-in-law for these our blessings.

[*Much laughter through the room.*]

This is the supreme moment of my life.
I thank our friends for their felicitations,
And hope you will visit us in Albany.

JOSEPH BROWN [*Tall, handsome, smiling eyes and easy manner*]:
Mrs. de Visme urged this double wedding —
Preferring to face one battle of the heart
Instead of two. Catherine and I invite you
To visit us often in Louisville.

PATTERSON [*Rising*]:
I'm very proud of my pupil, Aaron;
He has accomplished the impossible —
Finishing his law course in six months
Instead of the usually prescribed three years.
He has established himself in Albany
In ninety days as an astute lawyer.

AARON [*Rising*]:
I thank you, Judge Patterson, for your remarks;
But I must call attention to the fact
That my friend, Alexander Hamilton,

34

Also finished his law course in six months.

HAMILTON [*The handsomest and best-dressed man in the room, although only five feet, six inches tall, lifts his glass and smiles in a friendly manner*]:

Aaron found a way to open the door
And I merely followed his example.
My wife and I wish Colonel and Mrs. Burr
All the happiness due to ability
And which they both so richly deserve — also
We wish the same to Mr. and Mrs. Brown.

[*Much applause.*]

TIMOTHY EDWARDS:
I am proud to be alive this day
To say that my dear ward and nephew, Aaron,
Has been an honor to our family
By his legal accomplishment and also
By his achievements in the recent war.

[*More applause.*]

OGDEN:
Aaron and I attended Princeton together,
Then entered our country's service together,
And at Quebec came as near dying for it
As any two soldiers ever did.
May the bride and groom have much happiness.

[*More applause.*]

JAMES MADISON [*He is the same size as Hamilton; has the pale face of the student; bright hazel eyes; dressed plainly as a Quaker. He rises and lifts his glass.*]:

I also was at Princeton with Aaron,
And we his close associates admire him.
He will climb high the ladder of his choice.
We have spent delightful days at the Hermitage
And have come to know and greatly admire
These two most lovely and intelligent brides.

35

[*Applause.*]

JOSEPH BROWN:

My friends, we appreciate these compliments,
But Catherine and I must go at once.
We have fifteen miles to drive to the wharf.

[*The whole company rises and engages in a babble of
conversation, all flitting from group to group, exchanging felicitations with the brides and grooms
and gradually departing through the open door.
Aaron is seen shaking hands with his particular
friends, Hamilton, Madison, Timothy Edwards and
Judge Patterson. His sister, Sally Reeves, rushes up
and kisses Aaron, also his aunt, Esther Edwards. The
room is almost cleared, when Theodosia rushes in.*]

THEODOSIA:

Aaron, I must go upstairs with the family
And help dear Catherine close her satchel,
Then quickly change to my own traveling clothes.
But, darling, I shall return directly.
Here comes Matt Ogden for a final talk.

[*She dashes out of the room, and Aaron and Ogden
take chairs by the window.*]

OGDEN:

I wouldn't have missed this day for anything!
At last you have your wish. Your life has begun!
I hear that you have taken a lovely house
And have already many wealthy clients!

AARON:

Yes, it is all true. The wheel of fortune
Has turned my way! The New York Legislature
Is denying Tory attorneys the right
To appear in court. This fact and my army
Reputation have brought me far more clients
Than I can handle — so I pick and choose!
It is fantastic! My fees are so large

36

That I cannot find safe investments.
I want you to come soon and visit us.

OGDEN:
I shall indeed. Meantime I envy you —
Your health restored, your income now assured!
What are your plans for future undertakings?

AARON:
When the British are driven from New York,
I plan to make that city my headquarters
And to purchase Richmond Hill for my home.
Meantime, Theodosia and I shall find
Suitable husbands for her three daughters —
I shall make lawyers of Fred and Bartow —
Yes, I mean to accomplish worthwhile things!

OGDEN:
So far you have not failed to get what you want!

AARON:
Matt, you and I exchange our confidences
Which we could never tell to anyone else —
Let's keep it that way always! Tell me frankly
How long you think this war will still continue?

OGDEN:
The game is up! The British now are through!
I give them just six months to leave New York!

AARON [*Laughing*]:
I fear it will be somewhat longer than that.
Were I in charge they would have gone long ago!
Anyway, I mean to build up a fortune!

OGDEN:
How can you be so sure? You startle me!

AARON:
We're born just what we are! We cannot change!
I chose Theodosia because I love her.
Uncle Thaddeus had a million-heiress
Ready for me! The many lovely daughters

Of the Schuyler family, the Livingstones,
The Van Rensselaers, the Clintons and others
Were all expecting me to approach them!
I have proved that I am not mercenary.
I will be more constant to Theodosia
Than I could be with anyone else.
She is without a peer among women!

[*A voice is heard from the hall.*]

MRS. OGDEN:
Matt, the stage is at the gate. Do come at once!

[*Aaron and Ogden walk toward the door, Aaron holding back.*]

AARON:
This is the most important day in all my life.
The son of Aaron Burr and the grandson
Of Jonathan Edwards, both most brilliant men,
Has by this marriage proved to all the world
That he needs no other staff to lean upon!
Unlike Alexander, I am legitimate,
And need no wife to bolster up my prestige!
I shall alone control my destiny!
My wife will be subservient to my will!
She will respond to all my slightest whims!
Like Caesar and Frederick, my star will shine!
I shall go down in history, a great man!

[*Theodosia enters the room as Ogden, looking troubled by Aaron's outburst, dashes out. She is dressed in a becoming blue traveling dress, a blue bonnet with pink ribbons which match her flushed cheeks. She rushes up to Aaron and they put their arms around each other and fervently kiss.*]

THEODOSIA:
Aaron, my darling, what have you been doing?
They have all gone. Mother and the children
Have been upstairs waiting for you to come.
Please have Carlos finish your bags and bring them.

38

Then we can all enjoy a few moments
Together before we start on our new life.
Oh, Aaron, it is all so wonderful!
Your friends are all so fond of you, my dear!

AARON:
Yes, Theodosia, I am satisfied!
This day will mark the beginning of my career,
And nothing will ever interfere with it!
I have been telling Matt what it means to me —
Our love, our marriage, our understanding!
I'm the happiest man in this whole world,
And I promise to bring great fame to my dear wife!

THEODOSIA:
And I'm the happiest woman in the world!
Nothing ever can or will come between us!
Now run at once and get ready for the boat!

[*Aaron kisses her and hurries from the room as Mrs.
de Visme joins her daughter.*]

MRS. DE VISME:
He is indeed a very happy man.

THEODOSIA:
Yes, he is happy, but expects too much.
How can I guard him from the world's pitfalls?
He seems too sure! He is too sensitive!
He will not cooperate with his friends!
He and he alone must have the final say!
I shall not cross him by a single word —
That is our only chance for happiness!
Thank God he loves my children as his own!
His pride of race absorbs his every thought!
He expects a progeny of geniuses
To carry on his name! I'll do my part!

[*Aaron and the children now rush into the room,
and Carlos puts the bags and two small trunks by the
door as the family gathers in a group saying goodbye to the bride and groom.*]

THEODOSIA:
Mother, dear, remember you are coming soon,
With all the children, to our new home.
Please don't feel lonely! We shall soon write!

AARON [*Giving each of the children a hug*]:
I have planned a dozen surprises for you.
Take care of your grandmother. Let no one grieve!
Remember that we shall be together soon.

[*Carlos takes out the baggage to the carriage, as they all talk together going through the door into the hall. Their voices echo laughter and happiness.*]

CURTAIN

# ACT TWO

## SCENE ONE

SCENE: *Aaron's house in Maiden Lane. Seven years have elapsed. It is late afternoon of an October day in the year 1789.*

*A bright log fire gives the drawing room a glow. The crystal chandelier sparkles from its multiple candles which have just been lighted. The whole room is bathed in a soft light which is reflected from the gilt frames of several ancestral portraits, and is mellowed by the handsome furniture with brocade and needlepoint upholstery. It is a long room — a spinet in one corner. The green brocade curtains have not yet been drawn, but the light from the outside is fading as the sun goes down. It is a picture of peace and grandeur. The bronze clock on the*

41

*mantel points to 5:30. The tall cheval mirror on the
wall reflects the burning logs.*

*Aaron is seated by the fire, and on a chair close by
his side is his little daughter, Theodosia, six years
of age. She is a pretty child with hazel eyes and is
becomingly dressed in pink and blue flowered crino-
line, with white ruffles around the neck and cuffs.
Aaron is immaculate in black velvet coat, white silk
breeches, black silk stockings, flowered waistcoat and
white stock. He wears low black shoes with silver
buckles and a powdered wig. He is carefully scruti-
nizing a note book, and Theodosia now rises and
leans over his chair with expectancy shown in her
manner.*

AARON:
Darling, I am proud of your progress in French.
I find that this translation is almost perfect.
I have marked in the margin a few corrections.
Mademoiselle will be quite proud of her pupil.
Now let me see the samples of your English,
Also your spelling and arithmetic.

THEO:
I did not bring down anymore of my notes.
Ma said your friends were coming to dinner
And you wouldn't have time to see all my work.

AARON:
That is true, and I should like to have you stay
A few minutes after the first guests have come.
I want you to be a woman of the world,
And it is best to start now to meet people —
The kind of people who make up our world.

THEO:
Are Colonel and Mrs. Hamilton coming?
I like them, especially Mrs. Hamilton.

AARON:
Yes, they will be here, and many others —

42

Mrs. Hamilton's father and mother.
General and Mrs. Schuyler, and many more
Important people, but none more important
Than my darling little daughter, Theo.

[*Theodosia hugs him around the neck and looks at
him with admiration.*]

THEO:
Will you have time to look at my spelling
And my arithmetic tomorrow?

AARON [*Patting her hand on his shoulder*]:
Of course, I shall. Now run along, dear,
And tell your mother I want to see her.

[*Theodosia gives him a kiss, takes her book and goes
out of the room. Aaron looks into the fire with his
chin in his hand and his elbow on the arm of the
chair, and reviews his recent progress.*]

AARON:
To think that seven speeding years have passed
Since Theodosia and I were married!
This last year she has suffered constant pain.
I see her pallor growing, month by month.
Yet she is brave and tries to do her part.
She measures up to everything I hoped for,
Except this malady which saps her strength —
And then her failure to bring forth my son!
Poor darling, she has suffered much for me.
Triumphant was our life in Albany —
I count it eighteen months of utter bliss.
My friends have filled my heart with happiness.
The British fleet left New York six years ago.
I came at once to live in Maiden Lane.
My New York clientele grew rapidly.
I've never lost a case in any court.
When I own Richmond Hill I'll be content!
[*Theodosia enters the room. Aaron meets her half-
way and leads her to the chair beside him. She has
lost all semblance of health and good looks. Her eyes*

43

*are still bright, but she is pale and thin, though brilliantly gowned. She takes the chair Aaron places for her.*]

AARON:

Our little girl has rapidly matured.
I shall make her a great lady and famous.

THEODOSIA:

She loves you dearly, Aaron, and obeys you.

AARON:

Now that your daughters are all married,
And both our boys so nicely settled at Princeton,
I can concentrate on little Theo.
Her governess seems all that one could desire.

THEODOSIA:

Yes, she's perfect and loves the child.

AARON:

How are you feeling tonight, Theodosia?
Sure you're able to stand this dinner party?

THEODOSIA:

Certainly! I am all right, darling!

[*Feeling in the pocket of her handsome lace party gown*]

I have come down without my handkerchief.

AARON:

I shall get it for you. Sit here and relax.

[*As he leaves the room, he pulls the bell cord on the wall. Immediately two slaves enter dressed in smart livery — a man who puts fresh logs on the fire and a maid who pulls the curtains across the windows. As they leave the room, Mrs. de Visme enters and takes a chair beside her daughter. Her hair is now snow white. She looks at Theodosia with concern.*]

44

THEODOSIA:

  I see anxiety in every glance.
  He thinks I am a hopeless invalid.
  Oh, well, I'll prove to him that I am strong.
  To purchase Richmond Hill has been his dream,
  But how can he pay off the mortgages?
  He owes more debts than he can well afford,
  And yet he does not worry! Why should I?
  An English butler and our housekeeper,
  Besides his drove of slaves! How can it last?
  But I will not complain — it's Aaron's way.
  I am the envy of our many friends.
  Oh, how I wish I had given him a son!
  He is a born instructor of the young.

MRS. DE VISME:

  In seven years he has made himself a power —
  To think he never yet has lost a case!
  He is acknowledged as the super-head
  Of his profession in this Empire State.
  He helps his friends and educates your sons;
  But for himself he has not saved a cent.
  I fear his lavish spending savors ill
  For comfort in old age and final peace.

THEODOSIA:

  Yet it seems there is nothing I can do!
  I dread his venture into politics,
  Instead of letting well enough alone.
  His nature calls for more authority —
  The example of Frederick is his bane.
  He wants to rule, or be the leading man —
  Surpassing Alexander Hamilton!

MRS. DE VISME [*Going to the door and peeping out*]:
  Two brilliant men like these must always quarrel,
  Although pretending to be honest friends.
  I wish the Lord would keep them separate.
  Men's politics is such a bitter game.
  Matt Odgen says already there is talk
  Of making Aaron Burr a Senator —

45

The ablest orator, his cleverest brain,
More influence than any other man —
These are the traits, he says, in politics,
Which spell success and party influence.

THEODOSIA:
The Union would have floundered on the rocks
Except for Alexander's subtle hand.
He forced assumption by the government
Of all the debts of all the thirteen states.
To pay this off he issued government bonds.
His party calls themselves the Federalists.
It stands for central government control,
While Thomas Jefferson extols democracy —
Divesting power into the sovereign states;
But Aaron has not aligned with either side,
And when he does the trouble will begin,
For Aaron is so fearless he will win.
Whichever side he favors cannot lose —
That is why he is so popular.
Both sides are courting him and always will.
That is his secret — that is politics.

[*At this moment little Theo and Aaron enter the room. Theo rushes to her mother.*]

THEO:
Mother, dear, the first carriage is at the door.

[*A footman in livery enters and announces the guests as they stream in: General and Mrs. Schuyler; Mr. and Mrs. Gouveneur Morris; Colonel and Mrs. Hamilton; Colonel and Mrs. Ogden; The Marquis de Lafayette; Senator and Mrs. King. As the welcoming begins, little Theo takes her place by her father, who introduces her to each guest. She makes a curtsey to each. They continue to come in quick succession — Baron Von Steuben; Colonel and Mrs. Nicholas Fish; Chief Justice and Mrs. Jay; Mr. James Madison; Mr. and Mrs. Edward Livingston; and Colonel and Mrs. Troup. They stand around in groups and are all gaily talking. Lafayette and*]

*Hamilton by accident find little Theo beside them.
Lafayette is tall for a Frenchman. He is now thirty-
two years of age. He is very dignified in his uniform
of a general, and smiles down on Theo, who smiles
back.*]

THEO:
Are you the man who gave us our liberty?

LAFAYETTE [*In astonishment turns to Hamilton, quizzically speaking in French*]:

What a remarkable little girl!

THEO [*Also in French*]:
I am just trying to be a woman
Of the world, to please my dear father.

LAFAYETTE:
My dear young lady, I was only one
Among thousands of your countrymen
And my countrymen who played our small parts
In bringing about the independence
Of the United States of America.
Our friend here, Colonel Hamilton, did much more
In writing your wonderful Constitution.

THEO:
I have heard my father say that he is
One of America's finest lawyers.

HAMILTON:
My dear Theodosia, there is no better
Lawyer than your distinguished father.

AARON [*Coming along*]:
Why, Theo, you have captured our two lions.
General Lafayette has just been elected
To the National Assembly of France.
We are fortunate in having him here!

HAMILTON:
Aaron, I was amazed when I heard that you
Had accepted the Attorney Generalship.

47

AARON:
  The truth is that from a monetary view
  I really should not have accepted it.
  Of course my law practice will suffer.
  My wife's sons will try to keep it alive
  Until I can resume it again.
  Having launched into politics last year,
  I hope this will prove a firm stepping stone.

HAMILTON:
  No doubt you are right. The future will decide.

  [*Then turning to Lafayette as Aaron goes to another group.*]

  I wonder what Aaron intends to do.
  He has won every case in which I was
  Involved against him! A very clever man!

THEO [*Looking up at Colonel Hamilton*]:
  Did you really write the Constitution?

  [*The two men laugh heartily, as Aaron happens to return in time to hear Theo.*]

AARON:
  It would not have been the same without him.
  The old Confederation was tottering
  And would have died an ignominious death
  Without the fine hand of Colonel Hamilton.
  And now, President Washington has appointed him
  The first Secretary of the Treasury —
  A truly great and deserving tribute.

  [*Theo's mother calls her to come over and speak to Mrs. Hamilton and the other ladies. Aaron passes to another group.*]

HAMILTON [*To Lafayette*]:
  Aaron and I at least agree on a strong
  Central government. He made wise suggestions
  In my desperate efforts to bring dignity
  And power to the central authority,
  Instead of giving all to the separate states.

48

LAFAYETTE:

What a strange mixture of brain powers you have
In America! Your precocious children,
Your wise statesmen, your independent leaders
In politics and military affairs!
I hope I have learned practical lessons
To take back to my beloved France!
The longer I stay, the happier I am
That I enlisted in your worthy cause.
I am not at all pleased with my recent news.
I am returning to Paris by next ship
But shall hope to come back when we are at peace!

HAMILTON:

We shall all miss you. What is this bad news?

LAFAYETTE:

On the fifth of this month, the Paris mob
Forced the king and his family to leave Versailles.
They have confined them in the Tuilleries!
Say nothing of this to disturb Aaron's party!
But you see why I must return at once!
I shall devote my life to help establish
A constitutional monarchy in France
Before mob rule ruins my dear country.

HAMILTON:

I see what you have gained in America!
You, Aaron and I have a bond in common —
The fear of mob rule by too much freedom!

[*They separate and pass to different groups. Several
ladies are seated together.*]

MRS. MORRIS [*To Mrs. King*]:

Did you see President and Mrs. Washington
In their chariot drawn by six white horses
On Cherry Street today, with out-riders?

MRS. KING:

I did indeed. No court in Europe
Could hold more august levees than theirs.

49

James Madison says it is going too far
For our new republic. Colonel Burr loves it!

[*The English butler opens the double doors into the
dining room and announces dinner. They all rise,
and Theodosia goes over to her daughter.*]

THEODOSIA:
Darling, you sit here until Mademoiselle comes.

[*She then goes over to Chief Justice Jay, and Aaron
offers his arm to Mrs. Jay, and leads the way into
the brilliantly lighted dining room. The two lustrous
chandeliers reflect the candle light from their glass
prisms through the open door. They all walk in
pairs, talking in a happy, friendly manner. Little
Theo remains in her chair looking through the doors
at the brilliant scene as the guests take seats around
the table.*]

THEO:
A woman of the world he'd have me be.
Well, I'm that already if this is it —
To dress in silks and satins, be at ease,
Smile and only talk of pleasantries,
To speak occasionally in halting French,
To quote what you have heard from senators —
Yes, that is being a woman of the world.

[*Snatches of conversation are heard coming through
the open door. They are offering toasts to "France,"
"The King," "Lafayette," "our beloved George
Washington, who declined to be a king," "our host,
the new Attorney General," "Alexander Hamilton,
our new Secretary of the Treasury."*]

THEO [*Listening intently*]:
To be a woman of the world is nice!
Perhaps I'll be a princess or a queen!
I can be anything I want to be.
I have it in my blood, my father says!

50

A WOMAN'S VOICE [*Through the door*]:
I'm surprised that Mrs. Croix is not here.
The men are all wild about her, it seems!
I hear she does not wear hoops at her levees —
Only clinging muslin. She's not a lady!

ANOTHER VOICE:
Perhaps she's a forerunner of women's rights!

ANOTHER VOICE:
Oh, no! Catherine of Russia is that!
Her victories over the Turks prove her supreme!

ANOTHER VOICE:
I hear our host believes that eventually
Women will be given the right to vote!

MADEMOISELLE [*Appears and hastens over to little
Theo*]:

Come at once, my dear. I am already late.
Did you enjoy meeting all the guests?

THEO [*As they pass into the hall*]:
I've had a wonderful time all evening.
I am now a woman of the world.

[*The ladies now return to the drawing room, and
their animated conversations drown out any individual conversation. They sit down in groups. Their
gowns are the triumph of London's art — brought to
New York by Mrs. Church — some apple green, some
autumn gold and some other vivid colors. Their pet-
ticoats show through the ruffled lace skirts. Some
ladies have large Italian gauze handkerchiefs, striped
with rainbow colors, tied around their necks. Their
hair is in ringlets — some powdered — built up to
different heights of grandeur. Their hoop-skirts are
of varying lengths and fullness. Their costumes are
all brilliant, but quite tame compared with the men's
creations. The men's coats vary from plum color to
cherry, raspberry, chocolate, dark blue and black.
Their silk knee breeches are white, cream or yellow.*

51

*Their black pumps all have sparkling buckles. Their
costumes might well put the peacock to shame. The
scene through the open doors in the dining room
is a riot of color. Laughing voices are heard as the
men take their seats again at the table.*

*The folding doors are now closed. The ladies' eye-
lashes are jet black and appear childlike when their
eyes are widely opened, but infinitely varied in their
expressions. Their skin is dazzling in its soft con-
tours. Their classic jaws portraying strength or weak-
ness, appetite or passive indifference. Their average
age is about twenty-eight — but for women endowed
as these, years have little meaning. It is a glorious
triumph of womanhood in America.*]

MRS. MORRIS [*Addressing Mrs. Hamilton*]:
   It was my husband who persuaded yours
   To write to General Washington last year
   That it was his duty to become
   The First President of the United States.
   I wonder whether history will give
   To either of them credit for this act!

MRS. HAMILTON:
   Well, my dear, what does it matter after all?
   Alexander seems to have a natural urge
   To start our country truly strong and great.
   He never thinks of history or credit.

MRS. MORRIS:
   But think of what a difference there would be
   If Adams, Madison or Governor Clinton
   Had been chosen as our first President!
   We all know, Betsy, that it was your husband
   Who persuaded Washington to accept the office.

MRS. JAY [*Whose voice is heard from another group*]:
   Theodosia, your dinner was delightful.
   We are all so proud of Aaron's success
   And hope it will continue now in politics.

THEODOSIA:
Thank you very much. I can't conceive
Of Aaron failing in anything he does.
I think that he was born with a charmed life.

MRS. KING:
I hear if Adams fails in re-election
As Vice President that Aaron will purchase
Richmond Hill, which he has loved since boyhood.

THEODOSIA:

I think such gossip is unfortunate
And that we shouldn't indulge in such a dream.

MRS. KING:
Of course you're right; all gossip has a sting!
I'm sorry I repeated the remark.

THEODOSIA:
That's quite all right. What difference does it make?

MRS. MORRIS:
I hope that Congress will not make Philadelphia
Our capital, although it's twice the size
Of New York City. What would we do without
Washington's chariot and six white horses?
New York is the natural capital!

MRS. KING:
Let us enjoy conditions as they are!
Politics is all a matter of trading!
Every politician's wife knows that!
There's nothing we can do but be prepared
To adjust ourselves, no matter what may come!

MRS. MORRIS:
It is absurd that Thomas Jefferson,
Late Minister to France, still wears French britches
And that threadbare brown coat, although appointed
Our Secretary of State! He must still be
A French Jacobin of the first degree!

MRS. KING:

He was the chairman of the wise committee
Which wrote our Declaration of Independence!
He thinks he now can do just as he pleases.
It seems that everybody wants to meet him.
Do you think he'll be at Washington's dinner dance?

[*The ladies' conversation is interrupted by the
double folding doors to the dining room being
thrown open and the loud bantering conversation
and laughter of the men drowning all other sounds
as they enter the drawing room. The men select their
partners for after-dinner conversations. Aaron and
Theodosia see that the slaves bring up chairs to seat
their guests, who form in groups or couples all talking at once in a chaos of sound.*]

CURTAIN

# ACT TWO

## SCENE TWO

SCENE:   *U. S. Senate, Philadelphia. The United States
Senate Chamber in Congress Hall, Philadelphia,
about 4 p.m., late in February, 1792, occupies the entire stage. The rostrum is at left, near front.*

*On the dais behind a long, massive mahogany desk
is seated Vice President John Adams. He wears a
short curly wig and soft white stock. His smooth
round face has good features, large intelligent eyes
and heavy eyebrows. On a lower level, two clerks
are seated.*

*Below, arranged in rows, are the chairs of the 26
Senators, each with a small desk in front of him.
Senator Burr's desk is in the front row, center. The
desks are arranged so that all the senators show a*

*three-quarter profile to the audience. A page boy has just handed Aaron a small package of letters. It is currently well-known that when not engaged in debate he spends much of his time writing to his wife and daughter, who were forced to remain at their residence at Richmond Hill in New York City on account of the wife's poor health.*

*Aaron takes from the envelope a letter and divides his attention between reading it and listening to the routine business being conducted by the Senate. Page boys are passing back and forth taking notes to the clerks' desks to be filed with the records, etc. A Senator in the rear to the right is standing by his desk reading a long communication hardly audible. Most of the Senators are engaged in reading and writing memoranda — only a few listening to the Senator's monotonous reading from his notes.*

THE SENATOR:
"By an Act passed the 27th of April, 1784, entitled 'An Act for the Settlement of the pay of the levies and militia for the services in the late war,' and for other purposes therein mentioned, the mode in which the abstracts for pay and subsistence are to be made out and settled is particularly pointed out, and competent powers and directions for the liquidation of those accounts are thereby given to the treasurer and auditor."

*[Addressing the chair.]*

I move you, sir, that this clause be passed
To the committee on accounting.

VICE PRESIDENT ADAMS:
You have heard the motion duly seconded.
All in favor say aye. . . Contrary, no.
The ayes have it, the motion is carried.

*[While this desultory reading was going on, Aaron has been engaged in writing rapidly on a sheet of*

55

*paper. He now picks it up and reviews it in a sub-dued voice.*]

AARON:
"My darling Theodosia, I received with joy and astonishment a few minutes ago two affectionate letters. The mail closes in a few minutes and I will scarcely have time to acknowledge your goodness. The roads and ferries have been impassable so that until now, no post has arrived since Monday. It was a knowledge of your mind which first inspired me with respect for that of your sex. In fact, I believe girls should have a college education the same as boys. Boys and girls are educated much in the same way until they are eight or nine and it is generally admitted that girls make at least as much progress as boys. Why then is it not thought worthy to attempt to discover the particular age at which the male superiority becomes evident?

"I do not like little Theo's indolence or the apologies made for it. I believe women have as good brains as men. By my experiments, I hope to prove it. Have my directions been followed with regard to her Latin and geography?

"I bless Sir John, who with the assistance of Heaven, has thus far restored your health. In the course of this scrawl I have several times been called upon to vote, which explains its incoherence. I am impatient to know whether writing long letters fatigues you. Dr. Rush thinks you should take hemlock, and that it has the narcotic effect of opium, super-added to other qualities. God grant that it may restore your health. Affectionately, A. Burr."

[*Vice President Adams is heard to say: "The ayes have it, the motion is carried," as Aaron picks up and reviews the letter he has written to his daughter, Theo.*]

56

AARON:

"At length, my dear Theo, I have received your letter
of January 20th, written a month ago. I observe it
was not put into the post office until the day before
yesterday. I suppose Frederick or Bartow put it some
place where it lay forgotten. It would have been a
pity that such a letter should have been lost. There
is something in the style and the arrangement of
words which would have done honor to a girl of
sixteen, whereas you are only nine. It indicates an
improvement, not only in style but in your knowledge of French. I have read it several times, and I
am very proud of you.

"Observe that the Journal of what you do is to be
sent to me enclosed in a letter every Monday morning. The following are your only misspelled words
in your last letter. You write accurate with only one
c, laudnam for laudanum, intirely for entirely. Continue to use these words in your next letter that I
may see that you know the true spelling. Also tell
me what laudanum is. Where and how made? What
are the effects?

"I beg, Miss Prissy, that you will be pleased to name
one unsuccessful effort which you have made to
please me. Learn the difference between 'than' and
'then.' You will soonest perceive it by translating
them into Latin. Now, let me see how handsomely
you can subscribe your name to next week's letter.
Your affectionate, A. Burr."

[*The session is drawing to a close. Aaron rises and
addresses the Chair. A stir passes through the Chamber.*]

AARON:
Mister President, I offer a motion.

ADAMS:
The Senator from New York has the floor.

57

AARON:
After the lengthy debates we have had,
My motion should be carried unanimously.
I move that beginning with the next session,
Our Senate galleries shall be open
To the public while the Senate is engaged
In its legislative capacity.

[*A voice is heard seconding the motion.*]

ADAMS:
Are there any remarks? I hear none.
Those in favor say 'aye', contrary 'no.'

[*A chorus of 'ayes' is heard, no dissenting votes.*]

AARON [*Thinking the time is ripe, again rises*]:
Mister President, I desire at this time
To report for our special committee.

[*Vice President Adams nods consent.*]

In the opinion of our committee,
And we believe of all Americans,
No man stands higher than the Honorable John Jay,
The Chief Justice of our Supreme Court.
He has been nominated by the President
As Envoy Extraordinary to Great Britain.
You appointed a committee to explore
The matter and report its conclusions.
We're unanimous that such an appointment
Is inexpedient and contrary to
The spirit of the Constitution itself.
Without reflecting on the integrity
Of John Jay, we offer this resolution:

[*Taking it from his pocket he proceeds to read it.*]

"Be it resolved that to permit the judges
Of the Supreme Court to hold, at the same time,
Any other office or employment
Emanating from and held at the pleasure

58

Of our Chief Executive, is contrary
To the spirit of the Consitution,
Would tend to expose them to the influence
Of the Executive, would be mischievous
And from every point of view impolitic."
I move this resolution be adopted.

[*A voice is heard seconding it.*]

ADAMS:
You have heard the motion. Any remarks?

[*Loud whispering is heard through the room, as
Senator King, with red face and exicted appearance,
rises and is recognized by the Chair.*]

SENATOR KING:
This resolution is ridiculous —
Although the committee is unanimous!
They must have been unduly influenced
By the specious arguments of their chairman!
To go contrary to the wishes
Of our beloved President Washington,
And cast aspersions on the character
Of our honorable Chief Justice is not only
Unbecoming but a direct insult
To our President and our Chief Justice.
Can anyone here conceive of John Jay
Being suservient to any living soul?
Can anyone believe that he would or could
Be a tool in the hands of our President?
Or that he ever would go contrary
To what he considers our country's interests?

[*He looks over at Aaron and takes his seat.*]

AARON [*Jumping up and waving his arm*]:
I am greatly astonished that my colleague
Should put into this case personalities!
I'm thinking only of what is for the best!
Should functions of our Justices
Be cluttered up by services abroad?

59

Should they be sent to carry out desires
Of him who had appointed them to serve
As Justices of that most august court —
The highest court of these Unted States —
Their duties prostituted and enlarged!
Thank Heaven in this case we need not fear!
But let us stop and think of future years!
Might not this court become a political club?
Think of what has happened to Tammany Hall!
To guard against such possibilities
This resolution now should be adopted!
Remember, we are setting precedents!
Let's rise above all personalities!

[*A general tense, emotional strain is apparent in all faces as the Senators look at Aaron. They know that if they adopt his resolution, they will offend Washington, John Jay and their consituents. They marvel that Aaron has taken such an impersonal, brave stand. They know that it will injure his political future. They think, "How can politics be divorced from personalities?" The aisles are all filled with excited Senators whispering together.*]

ADAMS [*Knocking loudly with his gavel. All take their seats*]:

Gentlemen, are you ready for the question?

[*All remain quiet.*]

All in favor of the motion, please rise.

[*The members of Aaron's committee and three others rise — a total of 8.*]

Those opposed, please rise.

[*Eighteen senators rise.*] The motion is lost.

SENATOR KING:
Mister President, I move that the Honorable
John Jay be confirmed as envoy to Great Britain.

[*A voice seconds it.*]

ADAMS:
All in favor of this motion, please rise.

[*Eighteen stand up.*]

Those opposed, rise.

[*Eight stand up.*] The motion is carried.

If there are no objections, we stand adjourned.

[*As the Senators leave the room, several stop at Aaron's desk and shake his hand as a friendly gesture. Above the general conversation, a sentence or two can be heard.*]

A SENATOR:
We all know this sets a bad precedent.
If it had been anyone but John Jay
Aaron's motion should have carried. He's fearless!

[*Finally the Senate Chamber is cleared of all but Aaron. He is slumped at his desk. His brilliant eyes look into space.*]

AARON [*Muttering and pounding on the table*]:
I know I am right and they know I am right!
They are cowards — afraid of their shadows!
At least I have broken down the rule
That the public should be barred from our debates.
The Jay affair is quite a different matter!
Our country will suffer from today's action!
I tried to abolish slavery in New York,
When I voted in the State Assembly,
As an example for the other states.
I was right, but my motion was defeated!
If not abolished by legislation,
Slavery will someday lead to civil war!
What fools these men are who cannot see
Beyond the present age — and selfish interests!

61

[*Aaron's outburst is suddenly interrupted by Matthias Ogden, his old friend, accompanied by the colored janitor.*]

OGDEN:

I tried your office and your boarding house,
Then came here and literally forced myself in.
You sent for me and I came at once,
But you did not tell me where to find you.

AARON [*Shaking hands and patting Ogden's shoulder*]:
Dear old Matt, I knew you'd soon be here.

[*Turning to the janitor.*]

Thank you, Soloman, for letting my friend in.

[*They take chairs.*]

Matt, I badly need your moral support.
You know me better than anyone else —
Perhaps I should say except Theodosia.

[*Showing emotion.*]

The poor darling is doomed — cancer can't be cured!
I am a mental wreck, because I know
She will soon die! I want to resign
And go to her and sit by her side,
But she will not permit it. She does not know
Her condition and I cannot tell her!
What good could it do? I have lived only
To do something great for my country, and her!
My heart is broken because I can't do both!
She insists that I carry on here,
But they spurn my advice. I'm almost crazy!

OGDEN:

The same old Aaron! I remember Quebec!
You might have won but — the lack of snow
Prevented it! Now here it is again!

AARON [*Becoming excited, rises from the chair and*

62

*paces up and down the aisle while Ogden sits at the
next desk in sympathetic attention*]:

Yes, something always happens to thwart my plans.
What is it? Is there a personal God
Who is against me? I don't believe such rot!
I will win in the end and see this nation
Occupy this entire continent!
All of North and Central America!
We will bring Europe out of its misery
By proving freedom and democracy best!
Education of our people is the key!
I know this can't be done in my lifetime!
The foundation can be laid, and I will lay it!

OGDEN [*Laughing loudly*]:
Still the dreamer; still the little emperor!
Why can't you accept the world as it is?
You have the capacity to enjoy life,
Enjoy women, enjoy reading the classics —
Why not relax? We are only humans
And here for a very short time at best!

AARON [*Throwing himself into a chair and pounding
the desk*]:

You talk like a child! We are not put here
To live a life of ease, then die like dogs!
At least I am not — I want a better world!
No slaves, no thieves, no beggars, no murderers!
It can be done, Matt, if we forget
Our selfish motives and live for helpfulness!

[*He wipes his brow and looks at Ogden with despair.*]

OGDEN [*Calm but showing concern*]:
What has happened to cause all this emotion?

AARON [*Passionately*]:
They all hate me for being independent.
They cannot rise above personalities.
Think of sending our Chief Justice to England

63

To carry out political policies!
It makes no sense! It prostitutes the Court!
Our honored Justices should be confined
To the interpretation of the law.
John Jay has been my true and valued friend.
Now I suppose he will be my enemy!
Washington and Jefferson cannot see
What such a precedent may lead to!
They both think that I am untrustworthy!
Hamilton is even worse — and yet he hates
Jefferson even more than I do!
The trouble is, I do not knuckle to them!
I think about our country and its future!
Anyway, it is finished and I am sunk!
Yet I will carry out my own ideas
Of what is best for these United States
Even if I die for it — so help me God!

OGDEN:
Why should you worry? Why should you take the
    world
Upon your shoulders? You can't run the world —
And yet it seems that's what you want to do!
Why not be satisfied with your big niche?

AARON:
I can't! George Washington's fumblings
Drive me mad! He knows I look upon him
With contempt! He wants to ruin me!
The people look upon him as a god!
Anything I try to do for the good
Of this nation, he blocks through predjudice!
His is a small mind. He has fooled the world!

OGDEN:
History will forget his weaknesses.
As leader in our Revolution
And our first President, he will rank supreme!

AARON:
And he is supreme and has many fine traits,

64

But think of a President so predjudiced
That he denies me access to the files
Of the State Department with foreign states,
Thus preventing me from finishing my book
On the history of the Revolution!

OGDEN:

Did he really do that? You surprise me.
Jefferson must have had a hand in it!

AARON:

That is only one illustration
Of the way I have been humiliated.
Madison and Monroe presented
A request from the Senate that I
Be appointed Minister to France.
Washington refused and appointed Monroe!

OGDEN:

I must say you have been treated shamefully. . . .
You are suffering martyrdom at the hands
Of three most powerful and jealous men.

AARON:

Yes, you are right in putting it that way.
Washington has loathed me since I told him
Emperor Frederick's tactics eclipsed his!

OGDEN:

You are so outspoken, you offend these men!

AARON:

I know Hamilton can never forgive me
For taking his father-in-law's Senate seat
By turning Tamany Hall to politics!
I am not a member but they like me!

OGDEN:

How you do it, I will never understand!
I think you must be a miracle worker!

[*They both laugh heartily.*]

AARON:

    As for Jefferson, we see few things alike.
    The idea that all men are born equal
    Is preposterous, as any man of brains
    Must admit! And yet he insists on it!

OGDEN:

    The situation seems childish to me.
    You admire Hamilton but hate Washington
    And Jefferson. Washington admires
    Jefferson while Hamilton hates him!

AARON:

    You are quite right. We all four should be friends.
    We all desire neutrality with Europe,
    The extension of the United States,
    Taking Florida and Louisiana
    As soon as possible — and to this end
    That Spain must be driven from this continent!
    The navigation of the Mississippi
    Is necessary for this expansion!

OGDEN:

    Then why do these three men thwart your plans?

AARON:

    They are jealous and narrow-minded!
    We differ in methods of accomplishment!
    They want to postpone action! I would act now!

OGDEN:

    You are misunderstood, and always will be!
    Most humans are selfish, seeking food and ease.
    Few rise above this natural condition,
    And when they do, they are under suspicion!
    I think you take life too seriously.
    Why not be one of the crowd — love, laugh and die!

[*He rises and pats Aaron's shoulder.*]

AARON:

Matt, that is why I asked you to come here.

I want to be normal, but I just can't be!
Hamilton is my enemy. You warned me
Against him, yourself, a long time ago.
He tries to thwart me in whatever I do.
Is it jealousy or stupidity —
Or just fate? I defy them to ruin me!

OGDEN [*Again rising and showing concern*]:
Why worry if you are superior?
No, my friend, you are borrowing trouble.
Let us go where we can dine and laugh —
And forget needless responsibilities!

AARON [*Recovering his composure and rising*]:
You're right, Matt, come on! You do me good!
I do not know of an Indian wigwam,
But where is Jacataqua? Let us find her!

[*They laugh heartily and leave the Senate chamber
arm in arm.*]

CURTAIN


# ACT TWO

## SCENE THREE

SCENE:  *Richmond Hill, 1798. The library at Richmond Hill, Aaron's handsome New York home, is a
gorgeous room with its antique mahogany furniture
and bookcases which line the walls from floor to
ceiling. A portrait of his wife hangs over the marble
mantel. Aaron stands looking at it pensively. He is
dressed in a coat of maroon velvet, a double-breasted
Marsailles vest, white satin breeches, white silk stockings and black pumps. Full ruffles of white lace adorn
his wrists and fill the space between the long lapels
of his waistcoat below the white silk stock around his
neck.*

67

AARON:

You've been dead four years and I still mourn!
I must not be a sentimentalist,
For you are gone, my dear, never to return.
Thank God I still have Theo by my side —
A perfect companion, though just fifteen,
The perfect mistress of this spacious house!
I think I am blessed above all men.

[*He turns from the portrait and paces the floor.*]

Six years as Senator was quite enough.
I was defeated by the vicious plots
Of Hamilton and Jefferson, my foes —
With Schuyler reelected in my place.
And yet, I'm better off in many ways.
As member of the New York State Assembly,
I still can be of service to the cause,
And much more free to earn a competence
To pay the mortgage on this house and grounds
And give my Theo every luxury.
Enjoying friends, preparing for old age —
Yes, that will be my aim! And yet I think
What fools we are to let the Spaniards own
That fertile territory in the west.
Now is the time to claim that vast domain
Before the population is too great.

[*A colored servant enters and presents a card.*]

Show Senator Morris in. I'm expecting him.

[*A medium-sized, well-dressed individual enters the
room and is enthusiastically received by Aaron. It is
his long-time friend and admirer, Thomas Morris, a
member with Aaron of the New York State Senate,
son of Robert Morris, famous financier of the American Revolution.*]

AARON:

I'm delighted to see you, Tom; have a seat.

MORRIS:

    Congratulations, Aaron, on the passage
    By the Legislature of your Manhattan
    Company Bill. My colleagues, Samuel Jones
    And Ambrose Spencer, say it could not have passed
    With this odd banking privilege, without your skill.

AARON:

    The corporation could not have survived
    Just as a water company! I know
    We must have pure water, but more important,
    Another bank, with our expanding commerce!

MORRIS:

    Your trouble is, you don't defend yourself —
    You never meet your slanderers with slander!

AARON:

    I hope I'll never sink to that level.
    If our backwoodsmen are so ignorant
    That they cannot see that I seek the best
    For the country — well, I just can't help it!
    Someday they will find banks taking the place
    Of cattle and cowbells, land and whiskey,
    As the medium of exchange — and I hope soon!

MORRIS:

    They look on banks as a device of Satan
    For diverting their money into the pockets
    Of a few crafty individuals!

    [*They both laugh jovially.*]

AARON:

    I put some books upon your bedroom table.
    I hope they will amuse you. We dine at eight.
    Mrs. Croix is coming, also Talleyrand,
    Napoleon's Minister of Foreign Affairs.
    General and Mrs. Livingston, also
    Colonel and Mrs. Hamilton, and others.

69

MORRIS:

That sounds interesting. Your friend, Talleyrand,
Is a great admirer of Hamilton, I hear.
But Hamilton! Is he not your enemy?

AARON:

Hamilton and Talleyrand are statesmen!
I can't deny them my hospitality.
They both scintillate at dinner parties!
I also invited some younger friends,
Whom my daughter calls my "Tenth Legion" —
Washington Irving, Martin Van Buren,
Matthew Davis and also Billy Van Ness,
Who is a very brilliant federal judge.

MORRIS:

I hear of Mrs. Croix on every side.
Is it true that she is Hamilton's mistress?

AARON:

Now my dear Tom, you must not pin me down!
She fascinates each man she smiles upon —
With her lovely face and majestic carriage.
She looks just twenty-eight, but must be older,
As Lafayette was her first sponsor!

MORRIS:

I know it will be a most exciting evening.
You're the most popular man in politics.
Your thirty electoral votes prove that.
Next time you may be elected President!

AARON:

It was as unexpected to me as you!
I made no effort! If I were the President
I'd emphasize the importance of education —
Both for men and women — and as second,
I would acquire for the United States
This whole vast continent before too late!

MORRIS:

That is an Utopian dream — just like you!

70

You are the only man who can unite
The North and the South. You should be President!
Your friends are ardently devoted to you!
And remember, you have kept the party —
Now called Republican, not Democratic —
From breaking up! You've consolidated it!

AARON:

What a time I had with Governor Clinton —
He thinks Jefferson is not a statesman
And would do anything for personal gain!

[*Theodosia enters the room. She is now fifteen but looks twenty in her blue English riding habit, with black boots and a becoming black hat. She is about five feet, two inches tall, has a lithe figure and is very vivacious. She has sparkling hazel eyes, a square jaw and lovely auburn hair worn in curls over her forehead and ears. She rushes to her father and kisses him.*]

AARON:

Well, my dear young lady, you're home at last!
And just in time! You are my hostess tonight!
You remember my dear friend, Tom Morris!

THEO:

Of course I do! We're happy to welcome you!

[*Extending her hand to Senator Morris*]

AARON:

Tom, if you'll excuse me, I shall leave you
With Theo. I'll be back very soon.

[*Aaron leaves the room, and Senator Morris and Theo take chairs facing each other.*]

MORRIS:

Your father is extraordinary.
He wants to change and improve the whole world!

71

THEO:
My father has no faults — of that I'm sure.
His life is dedicated to a cause.
His whole concern is for these United States.
He feels he has a duty to perform —
To make this nation rise above the rest,
Superior to Babylon, Greece or Rome.
Improving on our English laws and codes,
Promoting peace and happiness and wealth!
Like the Chinese, he worships ancestors!
Confucius taught the brotherhood of man —
So did Mohammed, Christ and Aaron Burr!
I'd rather never to have lived this life
Than not to be the daughter of such a man!

[*Senator Morris, astounded by this seemingly occult outburst, rises and takes a few steps in front of Theodosia, but says not a word — just looks at her intently and then takes his seat, while she continues. She seems in a daze but her eyes are wide open and her head erect.*]

George Washington is honest but obtuse,
While Hamilton and Jefferson are tools
Of Satan to obstruct my father's path!
Ambition to excel and dominate,
By any means at any fearful cost,
Lies at the bottom of their characters!
My father will not stoop to answer slurs,
But fears the enmity of these three men.
And yet in silence he must carry on —
For this he thinks he came into the world!
Predestination is his ruling faith!

[*Senator Morris rises again and looks perturbed.*]

Insanity, you say — conceit or pride!
It matters not, since he was born that way!
His friends are legion, his enemies are few.
A day of reckoning is sure to come!
Someone must die and fill a martyr's grave!

My father's honor must not be impugned.
I live in constant dread! I cannot sleep!
He means not only life but heaven to me!
He was true as gold to my dear mother.
No husband gave more tender care.
He spends his life to make me what I am.
My languages, riding, fencing, art —
My education, religion, faith and pride
I owe to my dear father — him alone!
Dear God, make him supreme, and spare his life!
He holds it lightly at the price of honor!
One time he fought a duel with Mister Church —
His pistol was not loaded properly!
The second shot would certainly have killed
One of them; but Mister Church recanted
And apologized — but think of what a risk!

[*At this point Aaron returns to the room in his
usual brisk manner.*]

AARON:
   I hope you two have become acquainted.
   Run along, Theo, and rest before dinner.

THEO [*Jumping from her chair*]:
   I'll do so. I'm tired, but will be ready!
   I know there will be twenty-four guests.
   Senator Morris, I fear I have monopolized
   The conversation. Please forgive me.

MORRIS [*Rising and bowing to her as she leaves*]:
   I have been very deeply interested
   And hope that we will meet again quite soon.

   [*Turning to Aaron with vivacity*]

   Your daughter's a remarkable young lady.

AARON [*His eyes lighting up*]:
   She is my life, my happiness, my all!

MORRIS:
   I know she certainly adores you, Aaron!

You seem to win the people everywhere!
No man could carry more weight in Albany,
And your six years as U.S. Senator
Proved to all your rare ability!

AARON:
Come now, Tom, what's causing this outburst?
While in the Senate, I never lost a day!
I appreciate your encouraging words.
My closest friends have faith in my desire
To serve the interests of this country,
But there are a few who misinterpret
My motives. They have blocked my reelection!

MORRIS [*With emphasis*]:

No man of our generation is possessed
Of so much eloquence and forcefulness!
Your friends all hope you'll be our next President!

AARON:
My friend, I hope you will not publicize
Any such ideas! My enemies would say
We were conniving! Please be circumspect!

MORRIS:
I will respect your wishes, but I am sure
The Legislature would appoint electors
Who would vote for Aaron Burr to Doomsday!

[*Rising, looking at the clock*]

I'm happy to be here and know your daughter.
Now I must go and dress for dinner.

[*They leave the room together, talking in low tones.*]

CURTAIN

# ACT TWO

## SCENE FOUR

SCENE: *Office of the Vice President, Washington, D. C. It is May, 1804 — late in the afternoon of the last day of the spring session of Congress. The office of the Vice President in the new Capitol of the United States in the City of Washington occupies the entire stage. A large flat-top desk is in the center of the room, with bookcases and filing cabinets along the wall. There are a number of heavy chairs around the room. Aaron is seated at his desk, putting away letters to take to his home in New York. His secretary enters the room and announces: "Judge William Van Ness." Aaron arises to greet the judge. He is a medium-sized, vivacious, middle-aged man, one of the judges of the federal court.*

AARON:

    Billy, you're just the friend I need the most!
    To think that such a mediocre man
    As Morgan Lewis should defeat me
    As governor of New York is the last straw!
    I think I am politically finished.

VAN NESS:

    I came to you as soon as possible
    After the votes were counted and announced.

AARON:

    Alexander Hamilton at last has won!
    He has relentlessly pursued me for years.
    His slanderous pen has dug my open grave.
    My host of friends presumed to turn the tide,
    But they were helpless when I would not speak!
    They urged me to retaliate in kind.
    How could I when he never gave me cause?
    I could not call him "dangerous, insincere,
    A scheming hypocrite, a vicious liar,

75

Intriguing for a boastful Caesar's crown,"
Because I think him none of these vile things!
And yet he thinks that I am all of them
Nor hesitates to so express himself!
I've beaten him in every case in court!
I've beaten him in politics till now.
Jefferson's election was due to me,
For I alone could carry New York State.
I am the victim of a foul design!
My pride of ancestry has been my bane.

VAN NESS:

No one could have more devoted friends than you.
You are a statesman, not a politician.
Your two arch enemies have defeated you.

AARON:

Yes, they used the same tricks in Eighteen Hundred.
I see the electoral college tally —
February eleventh, Eighteen One —
As though it had been held but yesterday.
Jefferson and Burr each seventy-three votes!
Then Adams sixty-five, and Hamilton's man,
Pinckney, sixtyfour, with only one for Jay.
To think I permitted the election
To go to the House! I could have won it
By stooping as Jefferson did to trade.
But I remained in Albany, apart,
And saw my little Theo duly married —
While ten fierce days of balloting went on.

VAN NESS:

I was present at the inauguration,
But could not hear a word Jefferson said.

AARON:

One thousand persons packed the Senate hall.
Chief Justice Marshall administered our oaths.
The plodding Jefferson mumbled his address —
"We're all Republicans, all Federalists,"
Was all that could be heard, Theodosia said,

Seated in the center of the room.
Then followed my three years as Vice President,
Full of accomplishment for my country.
No Senator can say I've not been fair.
As presiding officer I've had their praise.
They honored and respected me to a man!
I surely would have been renominated
For another term except for Hamilton!
All in all, it has been a pleasant life.
Dolly Madison is my devoted friend,
Also her charming sister, Anna Payne —
And Betsy Patterson — all delightful.

VAN NESS:

No one in this new capital city
Has been more popular than Aaron Burr.

AARON:

Had Celeste become my wife, I'd be content.
Eliza, Clara and Leonora
Have each contributed to my happiness.
*The Morning Chronicle*, which I founded,
With Peter Irving as editor,
Has been an outlet for my roving mind.
Yes, the world has been a pleasant place!
And this, despite the snubs of Jefferson!
The people in my set are all refined
And shocked by Jefferson's vulgarity —
His dirty linen and his run-down heels!
The foreign ministers are all outraged
To be received without formality.
Yes, I've upheld our country's dignity!

VAN NESS:

You've had much to be thankful for, my friend.

AARON:

I have another year to carry on!
I should have answered Alexander's slurs,
But now it is too late to change my course.
He has gained the ascendency and ruined me —

And yet I know the God in Heaven is just!
I will fight life's battles singlehanded,
And in the end I'll win — for I am right!

[*He turns to his desk and takes a letter from one of
the packages, and again faces Van Ness.*]

Hamilton's slanders have caused both defeats.
Here's a letter he wrote in Eighteen One
To Congressman Gouveneur Morris, my close friend:
"As between Jefferson and Burr, the former
Without a doubt! As Burr in my opinion,
Has no principle, public or private;
Could not be bound by an agreement;
Will heed no monitor but his ambition —
And for this purpose uses the worst portion
Of the community on which to climb
To permanent power and crush the better part.
I know he's bankrupt far beyond redemption,
Except by those resources based on war.
He's wicked enough to scruple at nothing!
May heaven preserve us all from such a man!
Make any use of this that you see fit."

VAN NESS:
Yes, that finished you for the Presidency,
As Hamilton is a very powerful man.
And now you've lost the governorship
By Charlie Cooper's letter in his *Register*
Quoting Hamilton's speech all over the state.
Of course you have seen it. Here's the clipping.

[*Taking it from his pocket.*]

"Hamilton denounced Burr as dangerous,
A man not to be trusted in Government —
And I could tell you something even more
Despisable which the General expressed."

AARON:
Those malicious slanders in the papers
Are evidently believed by many voters.

Perhaps I should have answered them long ago.
Now it is too late! Perhaps I was too proud!

VAN NESS:

Here is a sample editorial:
"Has our Vice President sunk so very low
As to be insulted with impunity
By Hamilton? Why does he not reply?"

AARON:

Billy, it is very humiliating!

VAN NESS:

Well, what are you going to do about it?

AARON:

He knew I was about to call him out once!
He retracted by publishing a letter
In the *Evening Post*, to the effect
That he knew of no effort on my part
To intrigue to gain the Presidency.
Perhaps I should have called him out again!
I felt too sure of my position, no doubt!
Dueling is a relic of barbarism!
Why must we thus establish our honor?

VAN NESS:

Enough of them already have been fought
Over Hamilton's enmity for you —
For instance, John Swartwout and DeWitt Clinton —
But I can see no other recourse you have!
He has kept you from the Presidency,
And now the governorship, by vicious lies!

AARON:

Billy, you startle me! Perhaps you are right!
What a relief it would be to Jefferson
If one or both of us were out of his way!

[*They both laugh at this sally*]

Jefferson has entertained me frequently
And has professed his friendship, but has never

Appointed one of my friends to high office!
To think that James Monroe as minister,
Not I, has signed the Louisiana Purchase,
Still rankles in my heart! I would have rather
Brought that about than to be the President!

VAN NESS:
Aaron, your own career has been spectacular!
Your friends who really know you, adore you.
You owe it to them as well as to yourself
To demand that Hamilton retract his slurs!
He's had his day, but now has ruined himself
By attacking you, and I am sure he knows it!
That is why he has retired to the country!

AARON:
Billy, I confess I don't know what to do!
I respect what he has done for our nation,
And have nothing against him personally;
But this last slander is indeed hard to bear!

VAN NESS [*Angrily*]:
The whole world knows what he has done to you!
That miserable cur, Cheatham, Editor
Of Hamilton's paper, *American Citizen,*
Has attributed each of your advancements
To stealth, cupidity, fraud, foul tactics,
Bribery and swindling, and false vote-counting.
Thus far you have done nothing to refute it —
Except your letter to Governor Bloomfield
Telling him that all were vicious lies!
Your devoted friends do not think this enough!
The time's come to demand an apology!
A renunciation of all that he has said!
Why didn't you make yourself President
When you had the opportunity?

AARON:
Well, chiefly because I felt that the people
Wanted Jefferson. The twelfth amendment,
Thank God, makes such a quandary impossible!

Party government is far more logical
And safer than the original plan.

VAN NESS:

What do you think of "Honest Tim Pickering"
And his plan of saving the Federalists
From an influx of Republican states
Produced by the Louisiana Purchase?
He wants a new Confederacy, exempt
From the Southern aristocracy.

AARON:

It sounds like sedition, despite "Honest Tim's"
Background as a Massachusetts senator.

VAN NESS [*Rising and showing deep emotion*]:

Aaron, listen! I must tell you everything!
A senatorial committee of five,
Composed of Senators Pickering,
Hillhouse, Plumer, Tracy and Griswold,
Have sent me here confidentially
To ask you to become the leader,
As a highly patriotic duty,
Of a movement to save the United States!
They know you are the only man to assure
Acceptance by New York, New Jersey,
Rhode Island and Vermont. What is your answer?

AARON [*Showing emotion and deep interest*]:

I heard of this from my brother-in-law,
Tapping Reeve, who writes that Connecticut
Is seething and desires to separate!
I have not replied and will not do so.
We are living at a time of crisis!
What we do now will determine the future
Of the United States! I must have time
And consider every angle. To preserve
Our unity and make this nation
The greatest in the world is prerequisite!
I must see Jefferson, but rest assured
I never shall divulge your confidence!

81

VAN NESS:

   You have another year as Vice President —
   And besides these matters must simmer a bit!

AARON [*Rising and folding his letters and placing them in his satchel*]:

   I'm returning to Richmond Hill tomorrow.
   I had intended to ask my daughter
   And her son to visit me. Now I can't.
   Please tell your friends I must have time to think.
   There must be no Northern Confederacy!

VAN NESS:

   Will you demand Hamilton's apology?

AARON:

   Yes, and want you to be my go-between.
   I hope you can get his apology!

VAN NESS:

   I'll act with pleasure! You've been patient too long!
   Since you will be no longer in politics,
   What do you propose to do with your life?

AARON:

   That's what I want to see Jefferson about.
   If he will offer me a worthwhile office
   In diplomacy or a governorship,
   I shall take it. Otherwise I might use
   My experience to try to carry out
   What I consider my destiny demands!

VAN NESS:

   That sounds like the old Aaron! You'll need money!

AARON:

   I might try to raise money in Britain
   Or France! But all this is premature.

   [*Walking about in animation*]

82

First must come Hamilton and Jefferson!
Thirty days from now I may be dead!

## CURTAIN


# ACT TWO

## SCENE FIVE

SCENE:  *Weehawken. Duel between Aaron Burr and
Alexander Hamilton on the Palisades at Weehawken,
N. J., 6:30 a. m., July 11, 1804.*

*The rising sun lights up the broad expanse of the
Hudson River and the tops of the New York City
houses on the eastern bank. It is a magnificent view
from the Palisades. Richmond Hill is in the shadow,
but can be seen from the craggy elevation twenty
feet above the river, although it is three miles distant
downstream. Further on, the harbor of New York is
fading into the ocean. In a small level grove on the
rugged slope of the hill, wild flowers are growing in
profusion; stunted old trees are in full leaf and cast
their shadows on the dark rocks which form a se-
cluded, low-walled ravine which has long been a
favorite place for dueling. A winding path is seen
leading down to the river where a boat is tied up.
The attendant is seated in it, smoking his pipe.*

*In the grove on the slope, four men are seen in earn-
est whispered conversation. They are dressed in the
bright colored clothing worn by the gentry of the
day — long-tailed coats, ruffled shirts, silk colored
waistcoats and close-fitting knee breeches, and three-
cornered black felt hats. They are Colonel Aaron
Burr, who with an anxious and nervous manner
stands looking down the river, and Judge Van Ness,*

83

*Aaron's second, who holds a pistol case in one hand and an umbrella in the other — both of which he carefully deposits on a flat rock. The other two men are Matthew Davis and Marinus Willett, close friends of Aaron, in fact members of his little band of devoted followers. These last two have come to hide in the bushes and be ready to help carry their beloved leader to the boat in case he is wounded or killed.*

AARON [*Pointing down the river*]:
I think I see their boat now in midstream.
It is a long way off, so we must wait!

VAN NESS:
Aaron, you sit here on this flat rock
While we go out and tramp down the weeds
And clear a place where you and Hamilton
Can with greater ease step off your paces.

AARON:
Very well, but this spot is familiar ground
To me — and so is it to Hamilton.
Here I met John Church and Samuel Bradhurst.
And here I acted second for James Monroe
When he and Hamilton came face to face;
But no blood was shed on that occasion!

VAN NESS:
Aaron, we thought that you two had made up,
Because you joined in Hamilton's camp song
At the dinner of the Society
Of the Cincinnati on July the Fourth.

AARON:
Not at all! Anybody would have joined
In that camp song, "How Stands the Glass Around."
He seemed but twenty-seven, not forty-seven.
And very far from being the ailing man
He is supposed to be. He played a part!

84

VAN NESS:

    When they have landed it is my intention
    To meet them on the path, far down the hill,
    And see if I can possibly secure
    A brief apology at this late hour,
    Despite the many times I've tried before.

AARON:

    You are at liberty to please yourself.
    On two occasions I made him retract
    His bitter words. He may do so again,
    But I doubt it. We gave him every chance.

VAN NESS:

    Judge Nathaniel Pendleton, his second,
    And I exchanged more than a dozen letters
    Without effect. He thinks that Hamilton
    Is adamant because he's melancholy.
    He believes that he himself will die quite soon
    In any event, and so has brought himself
    To think his death would end forevermore
    All thought of a Northern Confederacy —
    Which, of course, would split this blessed Union.
    In other words, he wants to die a martyr!

AARON:

    I call this utter rot! It is the sign
    Of a bad conscience — nothing more nor less!
    He has maligned me now for many years.
    His spite has now become a habit of mind.
    I call this pose of his a brazen sham!
    He's gloating over his accomplishment,
    Since now he knows that he has ruined me!
    He is trying to clear his guilty conscience
    By grasping this excuse of martyrdom!
    All that he has to do, is be a man,
    Acknowledge his guilt and then apologize
    For his base conduct, and retract his slurs.

VAN NESS:

    Pendleton says he thinks in such event

85

That he would forfeit the respect of all,
As Commanding General of the Army.
He thinks his usefulness would fade away,
If he declines to fight this duel with you.
He has been trying to find a good way out
Without the forfeit of his pride, but failed!

[*Looking quizzically at Aaron.*]

Can't you devise some way to let him out?

AARON [*Looking distressed but determine*]:
I demand that he shall state in written words,
And publish it in some accepted journal,
That his remarks were based on politics
And not on truth; that he knows of no act
Of mine which could be called injurious
To our country's cause, or unpatriotic!

VAN NESS:
I shall relay all this and do my best
To bring about a reconciliation
Between our two most honored citizens.

AARON [*Looking down in excitement*]:
The boat has landed! They are getting out!
Who is the third man? He seems quite familiar.

VAN NESS:
It's Doctor Hossack, one of your old friends;
I'm very glad that they brought him along.

AARON [*Turning to Davis and Willett, who have been
standing aside in silence*]:

You two dear friends, please now conceal yourselves;
Hamilton should not know that you're here,
Especially if, in heaven's providence,
You can persuade him to accept my terms.

[*They shake hands with Aaron without a word and
withdraw into the bushes.*]

86

VAN NESS:
I shall go down the path and meet them there,
But you remain here and I shall report
As soon as possible. May God help me!

AARON [*Shaking the hand of Van Ness*]:
May God convert the heart of Alexander!
I hate this thing, but honor must come first —
It comes ahead of life! God be with you!

[*Van Ness disappears down the path. Aaron again
seats himself on the rock and meditates aloud, thinking of his past life, God and immortality.*]

My Theodosia left me in this plight.
I should be glad to join her in her grave
If I had any faith in the Resurrection.
What silly rot! Yet, countless millions feel
That Gabriel's trumpet will arouse each corpse,
Providing just a pinpoint on the earth
Where each may stand. What silly nonsense this!
The soul of man will flutter back to God,
His body lie a part of nature's soil.
What God will do with all these trillion souls
No man can tell! Immortality
Remains the mystery of the Universe!
Our span on earth is insignificant
Compared with trees and rocks and hills and stars.
They picture God far more than human flesh.
The Universe must be a mystery
Unsolvable by any human brain.
We live, we carry out God's plan, we die!
We have no more control than trees or mice.
Who sent us here? Who calls us hence? That's God!
But what He is and where He is, who knows?

[*Willett and Davis suddenly appear from the shrubbery, and Aaron turns to them.*]

WILLETT:
It's absurd that men like you should fight a duel.

87

AARON:

    One of us will likely die today.
    With him alive, I cannot far proceed.
    He blocks whatever project I may plan.
    His animosity I can't endure.
    He cannot be convinced that I'm sincere.
    He puts a false construction on my deeds.
    He thinks, or seems to think, that I'm a fraud.
    I've never stooped to answer his attacks
    Of jealousy and hatred and contempt.
    To do so I should lower my dignity.
    And yet, not long ago, he seemed my friend.
    I'd offer him my hand if he'd retract
    Those horrid slurs upon my character.
    I defy him to recite a single act
    That I've performed against our common cause —
    Freedom, honest rule by honest men!
    He will not meet me on a common ground.

DAVIS:

    His mind is now so poisoned with conceit,
    He holds himself aloof, superior.
    The absurd code duello is the vogue
    For proving men are honorable, not frauds!

AARON:

    Yes, one of us must die — I care not which!
    He robs me of each honor I obtain —
    Such is his strength and undue influence.
    I cannot live with him nor he with me.
    Perhaps it would be best if both are killed!
    If one survives he will be ostracized!

*[The shrubbery is suddenly parted and Van Ness rushes up to him in excitement.]*

VAN NESS:

    I can do nothing! He is adamant!
    Pendleton agrees that it is assinine
    For the commanding general of the army

And the United States Vice President
To fight a duel like ordinary men.
He thinks it will end duelling for all time.

AARON:

He probably is right. I hope he is.
At any rate, you've done the best you could
To bring about a reconciliation.
Let us get it over with! I am ready!

VAN NESS:

In case you're killed, have you a last request?

AARON:

I left minute instructions on my desk,
And a letter only for my darling daughter.
She's to dispose of all my private notes
Found in the six blue boxes in my room.
My estate will pay my creditors in full.
I am convinced that I am doing my duty.
I believe that Hamilton feels the same way.

VAN NESS:

Pendleton says he talked incessantly
Coming over in the boat, and he thinks
That he has done his best to avoid this duel
For the sake of his dear wife and darling children.
He said toward you that he has no ill will;
That in this hazard he has naught to gain,
But that your ultimatum he can't accept!

AARON:

All ridiculous! All childish babble!
Just let him put this hazard to the test,
Or retract his slanders of my character!
All the same, I wish it were DeWitt Clinton
I was to face instead of Alexander!
We can do nothing more! Tell Pendleton!

[*Van Ness motions to the three men waiting on the
path and they come forward. The two seconds care-*

89

*fully examine each other's pistols. Hamilton, dressed in all his finery, slowly approaches and joins the group. He and Aaron bow to each other politely and smile. Judge Pendleton is taller than the others. He is dressed immaculately in black, with white ruffled shirt. He and Judge Van Ness engage in whispered conversation regarding details of procedure, drawing of lots, etc.]*

PENDLETON [*In dramatice voice and drawing himself up to his full height and moving a few feet from the group*]:

Gentlemen, our side has won the drawing.
This gives to us the choice of the position.
General Hamilton will kindly take his place
At the extreme west end of the small clearing,
And Colonel Aaron Burr at the east end.
When I call loudly and distinctly, "Ready,"
You'll grasp your pistols firmly in your hands.
And when I call out, "Present," you will each fire!
In case both fire and no one has been struck,
I shall again call out, "One, two, three, fire!"
There will be only two shots fired by each.
Now, kindly take your places as directed,
Back to back in center of the clearing.
Take five steps forward, then both turn around.

[*Hamilton and Aaron immediately, without a word, take their places. Each takes five steps, then turns as directed.*]

PENDLETON [*Hesitating and showing emotion*]:
Gentlemen, my dear friends, are you prepared?

HAMILTON [*Slightly wavering and quite nervous*]:
Stop! In certain lights one needs his glasses.

[*Aaron remains cool and looks on contemptuously while Hamilton adjusts his glasses. Then both nod to Judge Pendleton, who mops his brow and with emotion proceeds.*]

90

PENDLETON:

Gentlemen. . . my dear friends. . . Ready!. . . Present!

[*Aaron takes deliberate aim. Two shots ring out in the sunlit atmosphere of the morning. Hamilton shot into the air. Aaron's shot has struck Hamilton in the right side of his chest and he whirls around and falls heavily on his side. At the same instant Aaron staggers slightly from the recoil of the heavy, smoking weapon. Judge Van Ness rushes up to him thinking he has been struck, but Aaron waves him aside. They both listen to the groans from Hamilton, who is now trying to speak. Doctor Hossack rushes up and rips open his waistcoat and shirt and attempts to stop the bleeding, while Judge Pendleton supports the stricken man's head as best he can.*]

HAMILTON [*In a dazed, halting voice*]:

Doctor Hossack, is this a mortal wound?

HOSSACK:

I can't be sure. A rib at right was severed,
The bullet slanted into your left kidney.
We'll get you home as quickly as we can.
Now swallow this laudanum. Try to relax!
The bleeding has stopped! A blood clot soon will
    form!

HAMILTON:

Not home! Take me to William Byard's.
He offered me his house in case of trouble.
My vision is blurred! Where did I put my pistol?
It belongs to John Church. Please send it back!

[*His voice grows weaker — the others gather around with solicitude.*]

PENDLETON:

Have you any final words to say?

HAMILTON:

I told you I would never aim at Aaron.
I hope he'll prove a blessing to our country!

91

[*Hamilton loses consciousness and sinks limp to the ground.*]

HOSSACK:
Now's the time to get him to the boat!
I'll take his shoulder. You, Judge, take his feet!

[*Aaron and Van Ness step up with hesitation.*]

AARON:
If you'll permit, we will assist you down.

PENDLETON [*With cold disdain*]:
We can't permit such desecration.
Please go at once. The General is light.
I can easily carry him myself.

VAN NESS:
Well, at least you're willing to testify
That the duel was fought by all the rules.

PENDLETON:
Yes, I gladly certify to that.

[*He then takes Hamilton in his strong arms and Doctor Hossack supports his feet and legs. They start down the path to the waiting boat while Aaron and Van Ness return to the flat rock. Judge Van Ness goes to find Messrs. Davis and Willett, who have been concealed in the shrubbery, watching the duel. Aaron is left alone to cogitate.*]

AARON:
My God, I hope he lives for both our sakes.
To kill a man, if unprovoked, is murder.
Why should our grievances create a duel?
It is insane by all of reason's laws.
I hope that this will put an end to duels.
I gave him every chance to say two words,
"I apologize." He did not mean a word
Of what he said. It all was politics.
My passions were aroused, my anger stirred.

92

We should have shaken hands and called it square,
Instead of acting like two lunatics.
But now it is too late; the die is cast.
With dignity I'll try to play my part,
And yet through life I'll hear those haunting words,
"This is a mortal wound. My vision grows dim."

[*Judge Van Ness and his two friends now appear and Aaron joins them as they all walk down the path to the boat.*]

## CURTAIN

# ACT THREE

## SCENE ONE

SCENE: *Blennerhassett Island, March, 1805. Blenner-hassett Island, in the Ohio River two miles below Parkersburg, West Virginia, is an island of about 300 fertile and well-cultivated acres. Extensive fields of green hemp are seen fading into the distance along the winding river bank. On the right of the stage the front elevation of the massive colonial house of Harman Blennerhassett, owner of the island, extends for about one-fourth of the distance from the front to the back of the stage. It is two stories in height, with tall colonial pillars based on the spacious veranda and supporting the overhanging roof. It is painted white with green shutters framing the eight windows — four above and four below — whose sparkling glass reflects the sun's rays.*

*On the left, a houseboat is tied up at the wharf. It is a substantial looking craft, sixty feet long and*

94

*fourteen-foot beam, roofed in from stem to stern. Stairs lead from the small deck in the stern to the flat roof, which is enclosed by a hand rail. A table and four chairs occupy the center. The entire boat is painted white. The trim of the windows along the sides is painted green, also the top of the deck. It is the houseboat which Aaron Burr had built at Pittsburgh from carefully prepared drawings and in which he and his friend, Gabriel Shaw, are proceeding down the Ohio River to the Mississippi and eventually to New Orleans.*

*Beyond the house and along the river bank, poplar and maple trees are coming into leaf, and wild grasses and low shrubbery frame a peaceful scene. A wellkept grass lawn extends from the house down the sloping ground to the river, with a broad gravel path between the house and the boat landing. In the center of the scene, beyond the lawn, are rolling fields and slave quarters.*

*Aaron and his hosts, Mr. and Mrs. Blennerhassett, are seated at one of the tables in earnest conversation. It is about two o'clock in the afternoon and the sun is high in the sky. The veranda is decorated with potted palms, hemp rugs and wicker chairs. Harman Blennerhassett is a tall, well-proportioned Irishman, with large blue eyes and red hair. He is dressed in homespun. He is forty years of age — nine years younger than Aaron. His wife is thirty-seven, very pretty and vivacious, with auburn hair and brown eyes. She is dressed in a becoming blue suit, fancy beaded moccasins, and wears no hat.*

AARON:
They said my usefulness was at an end,
But who are they to judge a superman?
I shall admit they seized the upper hand
While I was hiding from that frenzied mob
And trying to revamp my shattered life.

95

True, I neglected to surround myself
With strong-armed guards and methods of defense.
But I am far from finished. I shall prove
To all the world that I have just begun!
At forty-nine I have good health and strength.
My vast experience I'll use with skill.
My name will long endure in history —
When the names of Jefferson and Hamilton
Have moulded with their bodies in the grave.

MRS. BLENNERHASSETT:
It is by far the most exciting story
I ever heard. We both adore adventure!
You seem to rise above all handicaps.
Do tell us more — including all details.

AARON:
The hue and cry that went up from that mob
Of sycophants when Hamilton expired,
Which brought indictment for murder in two states
And caused my ostracism in the East,
Will not affect my western undertaking.
It did not thwart my conduct of the Senate,
Nor interfere with my deciding vote
In clearing Justice Chase from foul designs
Of Jefferson to impeach that righteous man.
It did not interfere with my reception
By scores of loving friends throughout the South,
Where gentlemen respect the code duello,
Nor with my happy visit to my child,
Where I rejoiced to see my grandson thrive.
My darling Theo ratifies my plan
To found an empire in old Mexico,
Then add it to the boundary of the States.
I gave Jefferson a chance to use my skill;
But Jefferson believes all men are equal.
He and I will always disagree.
Pretending friendship, he invited me
To a farewell banquet as his honored guest;

96

But now that Chase is cleared, he'll hound my trail
And trump up some excuse to have me hanged.
His cringing machinations I abhor.
So now, with God's help, I am on my way.
Now tell me more of your romantic lives.

HARMAN:

We've told you most of it. We're much alike.
Because I married my niece, the straight-laced folk
Of northern England ostracized us also!
We sailed to join the American colonies
Where every man is free. We bought this island
Expecting to make it pay before this time,
But, instead, my capital is being exhausted.
I must find a surer venture soon
Before it is all gone. We've reached a crisis!

MRS. BLENNERHASSETT:

Colonel Burr, Harman and I have spent the night
Discussing your proposal. We accept
And are ready to join your enterprise!

[*She speaks with vivacity and is broadly smiling.*]

HARMAN:

You are furnishing us the outlet that we want.
I've owned this island now for seven years.
We must do something desperate — and soon!

AARON:

You must decide this matter by yourselves
And not hold me responsible if it fails.
All is predicated on war with Spain.
I'm so sure of it, I'm risking my all.

HARMAN:

Who should know more than the Vice President!

AARON:

In that you err, for I am sure of nothing,
But war looks quite inevitable to me!
General James Wilkinson, governor

97

Of the Louisiana Territory,
Is expected here this day to meet me.
After seeing him, I'll know the facts.
He told me that the vast majority
Of the people of Louisiana are
Determined to drive all the Spaniards out
Of this whole Mississippi valley.

MRS. BLENNERHASSETT:

Did not the United States purchase it?
To me the whole thing makes no common sense.

AARON:

The trouble is, no one yet knows the boundary.
The Mississippi River is on the east
And Canada is on the north. As to the west,
Nobody knows! The viceroy of Mexico
Thinks the expedition of Lewis and Clark
Was really organized not to discover
The true source of the Missouri River,
Which is supposed to be the boundary,
But to set the Indians against the Spaniards.
Thomas Jefferson told our Indian agent
To "convince the Red Man of the justice
And liberality we guarantee,
To attach them to us indissolubly."
I saw these words myself — and they mean war!

HARMAN:

You're on the inside. We will join you gladly.
May we entertain your friend, the general?

AARON:

Thanks! I fear that that would be impossible.
He plans to meet me here in secret session
While his packet boat is tied up for recoaling
At Parkersburg. A rowboat brings him here
For an interview of only twenty minutes;
But, of course, I'll see that you both meet him.

98

MRS. BLENNERHASSETT:
He'll be surprised to see your new houseboat,
With its bedrooms, fireplace and modern galley.

AARON:
He will be even more surprised to know
That one hundred and thirty-three dollars
Covered the total cost of the whole thing.

HARMAN [*Looking incredulous*]:
You have the art of working miracles.

AARON:
No, like you, I am an adventurer.
We live a brief life here, then fade away.
We are living in a terrible age —
The age of Pitt and Napoleon in Europe,
The age of Spanish tyranny over here.
You and I are natural friends and partners.

[*He rises and puts his hands on Harman's shoulders.*]

We want our well-loved country to be free
From tyranny, and make it all one nation.

HARMAN [*Gazing into Aaron's eyes in excitement and enthusiasm*]:

Excuse me just a moment. I'll be right back.

[*He dashes through the door into the house.*]

MRS. BLENNERHASSETT:
Colonel Burr, you have completely won him —
His confidence, respect and loyalty.
God must have guided you to our island!
Harman is discouraged with his science
And astronomical discoveries.
Our slaves are not efficient farmers.
We trust our future willingly to you.

[*At this moment Harman returns, bringing a small wooden box, and hands it to Aaron.*]

99

HARMAN:
This small box contains ten thousand dollars
In United States money, which is all yours.
It is the first installment of our debt.

AARON [*Taking the box and looking into Harman's eyes with gratitude and surprise*]:
Harman, you have thrilled me through and through.
I hesitate to take so much till surer.
Anthony Merry, British minister,
And my close friend, has asked his government
For half a million for me when I need it,
Also for ships to guard us at New Orleans.
I am to meet my friend, General Jackson,
At Nashville just as soon as I can get there,
And he will lead ten thousand trained men
Into Mexico at the proper time.

HARMAN [*Rising and pointing up the river*]:
I think that that is General Wilkinson.
He has three oarsmen! He's in uniform!

[*They rise in excitement and look at the rapidly approaching boat.*]

AARON:
Come to the landing. I will introduce you.

[*They hasten down the gravel path waving handkerchiefs, and arrive at the wharf as the general's boat pulls up.*]

James, I welcome you to this our paradise.
These are my friends and hosts, all here to greet you.

WILKINSON [*Stepping out of the boat and shaking hands with Aaron and his friends and smiling broadly*]:
If they are friends of yours, they're friends of mine.

HARMAN:
General Wilkinson, our house is yours
Do come to the veranda for some tea.

100

WILKINSON:
   Thank you, my time is short and Colonel Burr
   And I have much to say. . . . Excuse me, please.

MRS. BLENNERHASSETT:
   Colonel Burr warned us of this. We'll go.
   It is indeed an honor to have you here.

WILKINSON:
   I shall hope to come back very soon.

   [*He shakes hands with Harman, kisses the hand of
   Mrs. Blennerhassett, and they both return to the
   house.*]

AARON:
   I have all in readiness — the maps and plans,
   Also letters from Merry and Jackson, too.
   Come to my sun deck. No one can hear us there.

   [*They ascend the stairs to the level deck and take
   chairs by the table.*]

WILKINSON:
   I'm sorry that I missed you at Pittsburgh.
   I came here at the first opportunity.

   [*Aaron takes his maps out of the box and spreads
   them carefully on the table. General Wilkinson, his
   epaulets glistening in the sun, is a large, ungainly
   man with high forehead, white wig, piercing black
   eyes set close together, like a fox's eyes. He glances
   at the maps casually, nods approval and then looks
   at the scene around him.*]

   Aaron, you possess the gift of fairies!
   Apparently you get just what you want!
   In one year after being Vice President
   You have explored both Florida and Georgia,
   Journeyed west on horseback from Philadelphia
   To Pittsburgh, where this boat was 'waiting you
   To float you down the river, by easy stages,

101

Stopping to make new friends along the way
At Wheeling, Marietta and Parkersburg.
In each of these towns, I have heard there are
From sixty-five to eighty substantial families
Living in stone houses where you're welcome.
And now, you're anchored in this Fairland,
Ready to move on to your new adventure —
The conquest of old Mexico! I admire
Your enterprise and your ability.
Now, tell me just what you want me to do.
I know I owe to you my appointment.

[*Aaron shows surprise at this unexpected opening
but controls his expression of face and manner.*]

AARON:

You owe me nothing. My success depends
Alone on you and Andrew Jackson.
You're both my friends. You know that I am loyal
And patriotic, having one desire,
To see the United States occupy
All of North America, in time.
To this end I have dedicated my life.
You know this from the days of old Quebec!
I've been thwarted by George Washington,
Hamilton, and now by Thomas Jefferson,
Who is so narrow, selfish and vindictive
That all his sins will find him out and crush him.
You and I know that the Spanish colonies
Are ready to revolt, including Mexico.
I know that I can lead them all to victory.
If war comes I'll accomplish this, my aim.
Now tell me, frankly, how soon will war come?

WILKINSON [*Growing nervous and fidgety*]:

I cannot say how soon, but war will come!
I know that Louisiana will revolt —
And that makes certain war in my opinion.

102

AARON:

Blennerhassett has volunteered to meet my needs
Till England acts, and that should be quite soon.
I look to General Jackson and his militia
For sufficient military support.
All depends on that. Now what can you supply?

WILKINSON:

If all goes well I'll send six hundred troops
To join you at New Orleans when you're ready.
I think that Jackson could send many more.

AARON [*Showing satisfaction*]:

With such a nucleus, I am content.
Your assurance is most welcome at this time;
I can easily raise the balance that I need.
Guard doubly carefully our ciphered code —
Only thus can we communicate safely.

WILKINSON:

Have no fear on that score. We'll meet soon.
Tell me more about your Washita Purchase.

AARON:

It is our safety valve! The contract's signed.
It calls for four hundred thousand acres of land,
Purchased from Charles Lynch for fifty thousand.
Easy of access! But two hundred families
Must be settled there within a given time.

WILKINSON:

You seem prepared for all contingencies.

AARON:

Exactly! I plan training my recruits
On this island for war and also farming.
If war is not declared, they will be settlers.

WILKINSON:

Splendid! As I am commander-in-chief,
I have the power to strike when you are ready.
We have been comrades now for thirty years.

103

AARON:

Yes, ever since our retreat at old Quebec.
This time it will be advance and not retreat!

[*Both rise and Wilkinson takes an envelope from
his pocket and hands it to Aaron.*]

WILKINSON:

Give this to Daniel Clarke at New Orleans.
He's rich and will invest quite heavily.
The Catholic bishop also will help you.

[*Then handing him another envelope.*]

And this is Jackson's splendid proclamation.
I must go now. Will meet you soon at Nashville.
Just let me know the day when you arrive.

AARON:

If only war comes, our success is sure.
Excuse me one minute, I must give you
Another page of code words I've prepared!

[*He dashes down the stairs.*]

WILKINSON [*Looking at Aaron with disdain, mutters*]:

Conceited fool! He thinks that I would serve
Under him in some subvient role!
I'd rather die! Conceit has driven him mad!
I am the man to conquer Mexico,
And when the time is ripe I'll do it, too!
I'll let him go ahead — prepare the ground.
Through Jefferson I'll easily find a way
To quickly put this braggart in his place.

[*Aaron returns with an envelope and hands it to
Wilkinson, who puts it in his pocket.*]

AARON:

Guard it safe, and thanks again for coming.
Can we be sure of Jackson's full support?

WILKINSON:

Perfectly sure, and he is fond of you.

104

[*He hastens down the stairs and motions the men in the skiff to get ready, then calls to them.*]

Boys, we must not keep that packet waiting.

[*He shakes hands with Aaron, steps quickly into the skiff, and it darts away. Aaron waves farewell salutation, then returns to his sun deck, puts away his maps and walks fore and aft, cogitating.*]

AARON:

Had I the funds, I could be Senator
Or President — he said anything I want.
I know I have the brains and common sense.
I know I have the people on my side.
They do not realize that Washington
And Jefferson and Hamilton combined
To thwart my progress. I defy them all!
My trouble is, I cannot save a cent.
I earn tremendous fees and lose them all
In speculation, entertaining friends —
And entertaining far beyond my means.
Well, what of that! We only live to prove
The influences of heredity.
My wife adored me and my daughter lives
To prove to all the world that I'm her God!
At forty-nine I have accomplished more
Than most men have at any age of life.
Shall I succumb or shall I carry out
My destiny like Frederick and Napoleon?
This Mexican adventure gives me zest.
If only England will supply the funds!
And yet, I fear a flaw in Wilkinson.
He was accused of plotting with Miro,
The Spanish governor of Louisiana,
To gain Kentucky for the Spanish cause.
He was held guiltless! Who am I to judge?
I know he has a thirst for wealth and fame.
Can such a man be trusted? I'm disturbed!
His eyes are shifty. . . . I must risk a chance.
I must be cautious. He could ruin me!

[*Aaron stops at the approach along the gravel path of Mr. and Mrs. Blennerhassett. They look up at him expectantly.*]

AARON [*Calling to them as he descends*]:
I shall join you at once. My plans are formed.

MRS. BLENNERHASSET:
We can hardly wait to hear just what he said.

AARON:
He feels sure that war will soon be declared,
And approves of our Washita Purchase.

HARMAN:
Then all is well. Our fortunes now are made!

AARON:
Wilkinson pledges six hundred trained troops,
And says Jackson will send two regiments.

[*They have reached the veranda and take seats. The sun is now low in the western sky. A slave boy places glasess on the table and a bottle of wine, which Harman pours out in excitement.*]

HARMAN [*Raising his glass*]:
Here's to the success of our great enterprise.

[*A skiff containing a slave oarsman and Aaron's companion, Gabriel Shaw, ties up at the float. Gabriel holds up a string of fish he has caught and then joins the company on the veranda.*]

HARMAN [*To Gabriel*]:
That is a fine catch. We'll have them for supper.

[*The slave boy carries the fish around the house to the kitchen.*]

You have come in time to drink a toast
To the early conquest of old Mexico.

[*Offering him a chair and a glass.*]

106

SHAW:
We saw the boat go speeding up the river.

[*Then looking at Aaron.*]

Was the general's visit a success?

AARON:
Yes, it was quite satisfactory.
He says that General Jackson expects us soon
At Nashville after visiting New Orleans.
So we must start at sunrise. Tell the boatmen.

[*He takes a paper from his pocket.*]

Here is General Jackson's proclamation
To his troops, the Tennessee Militia:
"The menacing attitude of the Spaniards,
Already encamped within the limits
Of the United States government,
Requires our Militia to be ever ready
For instant duty when they're called upon."

HARMAN:
It seems that war has now almost begun.

AARON:
But we must wait until it is declared.
We then will add the entire territory
Of the Southwest to the United States —
Mexico and clear to California!
Meantime tell them all that our objective
Is to colonize the Washita Lands.
That in itself is a worthy motive.
This island would be perfect headquarters
For training our recruits for war or farming.

HARMAN [*Looking at his wife*]:
I have no objection. Have you, Margaret?

MRS. BLENNERHASSETT:
It sounds exciting! Just what is involved?

107

AARON:

I'd send militiamen to drill recruits,
And well-trained farmers, carpenters and herdsmen,
And other craftsmen to teach other things —
Building houses, tending cattle and sheep —
To settle on the Washita homesteads.
There should be many millions in this venture!

HARMAN [*Looking at his wife, who nods her head in approval*]:

We agree, but what about Mexico?

AARON:

That conquest would start when war is declared.
Our settlers would become soldiers at once.
It is all very simple if war comes.

[*Stars are now seen in the sky. The windows of the Manor House, also of Aaron's ark, become lighted one by one by the candles within. The conversation on the veranda becomes a babble. The colored butler opens the doors and announces supper. The crystals of the chandeliers glisten through the open doors. Harman and his guests rise and go into the house together, all talking in excitement over the vision of the future.*]

CURTAIN

# ACT THREE

## SCENE TWO

SCENE: *The town of Nashville, Tenn., August 13, 1805. On the right, the facade of "The Hermitage," the spacious colonial house owned by General Andrew Jackson. It has tall white columns and two-*

*story porticos. At center, a level green lawn under tall live oaks whose branches shade the chairs and table under the trees from a bright sun. On the left, a gate in a white paling fence opening on a lane.*

*Aaron Burr is seated at the table and is reading aloud from the letter he is engaged in writing to his daughter, Theodosia:*

AARON:
"I'm still at Nashville and I love it here.
For one week I've been lounging at the home
Of my dear friend, General Jackson, who now heads
The state militia. He's intelligent,
Impetuous and frank, and appeals to me
As honest, patriotic, also wise!
His wife is very lovely. They've no children.
His two young nieces are a perfect joy.

"I'm glad to say I'm through the wilderness —
About four hundred miles of hidden trails! —
I was reduced to drinking puddle water
With green scum on the top, but here I am,
Alive and well, with these most gracious people.
They gave me a parade and public dinner
To prove their faith in what I'm doing.
Tomorrow I hope to move to Lexington
In General Jackson's handsome, sturdy boat.
There I join my 'ark' for New Orleans.
It all is settled country. I shall dine
With leading citizens along the way.
My custom is to send them word I'm coming.
They receive me cordially and with distinction.
The first toast is always to you, my dear.
They know you are the center of my life."

*[He is interrupted by the sound of trotting horses. The sound dies out suddenly as the horses are being tied by their riders, who jubilantly enter through the gate and rush up to Aaron. He rises to greet them. One is his host, General Andrew Jack-*

109

*son, a tall, lank, uncouth individual of thirty-eight, with long locks of sandy hair, hanging over his pock-marked face, and a queue down his back tied in an eel-skin. His manner and deportment are those of a rough backwoodsman. His black riding boots contrast with his tan leather breeches and long-tail coat. He shows by his large head and long chin and flashing blue eyes that he is a man of passion, and arbitrary decision — a typical frontiersman. The other is General James Wilkinson, commander-in-chief of the armed forces of the U. S. A., dressed in a full military costume, with epaulets and riding boots.*]

JACKSON:
Colonel Burr, that public dinner for you last night
Will prove historic through the years to come.
Your fine address has made a deep impression.
You have the public with you to a man.
I'm deluged with requests to keep you longer.

AARON:
I thank you from my heart for your good wishes.
My conscience tells me I must go at once.
As you know, I've waited for my daughter.
Your generous hospitality will stir
My heart with pleasant, lasting memories.
The boat that you have put at my disposal
Must not be kept in idleness a day.
I'll start tomorrow morning for New Orleans.

WILKINSON:
I told the general you could have my barge.
It's well equipped and carries ten strong oarsmen.

AARON:
My friend, you are most kind, but General Jackson
Has spared no pains to have his boat prepared
For Shaw and me; but know that I am grateful.
When we three have our meeting in December,
At New Orleans, the world will hear from us.
By that time surely all will be prepared!

110

WILKINSON:
What are the latest messages from England?

AARON:
I was assured just recently by Merry
That England will contribute a large fleet
To reach New Orleans as soon as we are ready.
I told him that December was the time.

WILKINSON:
For our success that fleet is necessary.

AARON:
What's delaying Jefferson's proclamation?
When he ordered you to drive the enemy
Beyond the Sabine, it was tantamount
To declaring war! The match is in your hands.
Ignite it, and the conflict will begin.
The Mexican adventure lies with you.
My recruits are all expecting action.

WILKINSON [*Becoming fidgety and embarrassed*]:
I have explained to you my difficulties.
I cannot fathom Jefferson's strange mind.
I have dispatched my troops to our frontier
And shall go there myself at his request.
I now expect a message any day,
And shall keep you well informed the hour it comes.

JACKSON:
You both know where I stand. I'm ready now
For instant action! I have written the President
That when the enemy shot down our flag
At New Orleans, the people everywhere
Thought that meant war, and that I stood prepared
To serve my country! Why does he delay?

AARON:
You told me his reply was favorable.
That was why I ventured to express
My opinion at the public dinner last night.

111

JACKSON [*Takes the letter from his pocket and reads it*]:

Here is what he says: "Always a friend of peace,
I am unwilling ever to disturb it
While our rights and interests can be preserved;
But when aggressions justify a war,
We'll meet our duty and convince the world
That we're honest friends and brave enemies."

AARON:

That certainly gives to James the power to act.
If Jefferson means he only will remain
On the defensive, he would make it clear.
He meant to act when Spain cut down our flag!

JACKSON:

I must say I agree with you most heartily.
We now are free to force a war on Spain.
General Wilkinson, are you prepared to act?

WILKINSON:

I feel that I must wait for further orders.

[*A noise is heard at the gate as another horse is tethered and a third man arrives — an officer in uniform. They all stand up.*]

JACKSON:

This is General John Adair, just come.
I asked him to this conference because
He knows the situation and is wise.

ADAIR:

I'm sorry that I had to miss your dinner.

[*Looking at Aaron.*]

The people are stirred up by your address.
May I ask the gist of your remarks?

AARON:

I publicly announced my long ambition
To lead an expedition into Mexico,

112

And that I felt quite sure our President
Would find it proper to declare a war.

JACKSON:
The country as a whole is ready now,
And Aaron is the man to bring success.

ADAIR:
But what if Jefferson should never act?

AARON:
I then explained my second undertaking,
To stake out homesteads on a fertile tract —
Four hundred thousand acres of rich soil —
Preparing settlers from the East and West —
A very great adventure in itself.
If war with tyrannous Spain is not declared,
My young recruits would earn this rich reward.

ADAIR:
I'm fascinated by both undertakings.
However, it seems that you have enemies!
I brought this clipping from the *Western World*,
Which, as you know, is published at Frankfort, Ken-
    tucky.

AARON:
Please, read it. I have heard many rumors.

ADAIR [*Reading the newspaper clipping*]:
"The project of Colonel Burr if accomplished,
Will not only unite the Spanish provinces
With all the western part of the United States,
In one vast empire, headed by himself,
But will change the world's political history,
Equaled only by Napoleon's empire."

[*After hearing this, all three look to Aaron for his
reaction.*]

AARON:
Such exaggerations are ridiculous!
Such fabricated gossip I despise!

113

My friends who've heard me speak, will always trust
me.
If war's declared, I'll conquer Mexico!
If not, I shall develop "Washita Lands."

JACKSON:
You have made your intentions quite clear.
As for me, war cannot come too soon!

AARON [*Looking directly at Wilkinson*]:
Our friend has ample power to act at once.

WILKINSON [*Looking at Aaron*]:
Just give me time! December's soon enough!
Get your fleet to New Orleans at once.

JACKSON:
The West is ready! Here are last night's toasts:

[*Looking at Adair as he reads.*]

"To the Mississippi's unimpeded current —
Our highway to the markets of the world."
"May the tree of liberty soon flourish
On the ruins of tyranny and despotism."
These are typical. There're many more!

ADAIR:
I believe that Jefferson would be most grateful
If Colonel Burr brings all this territory,
Now held by Spain, into the United States.

JACKSON:
My feeling is he wants some other leader.

AARON:
If that is true, why does he not say so?
I've gone too far to quit, since England is ready
To send her cruisers. Commodore Truxtun is ready
To blockade Vera Cruz. You two are ready.
And Comfort Tyler is training my recruits!
What other man could Jefferson select?

114

JACKSON:
I hope these newspaper calumniators
Will not make him suspicious of your actions.
Grand jury trials have cleared you in Kentucky,
Also in Indiana and Ohio.

AARON:
I have no fear, because I'm innocent.

WILKINSON [*Growing nervous, rises*]:
Gentlemen, I am sorry but I must be going.

AARON [*Looking into Wilkinson's eyes as they all stand up*]:
We're in your hands, James, and we've reached a
  crisis!
I'll keep you posted. Are my code words clear?

WILKINSON:
Perfectly clear. Just let me know when you'll arrive.

JACKSON:
The boat is ready. We are sure to win.

[*They all shake hands and walk to the gate. Jackson,
Wilkinson and Adair go out and Aaron returns to
the table, sits down and takes up the letter he is writing — then looking into space, meditates aloud.*]

AARON:
I feel I am surrounded by false friends.
Adair and Jackson I can count upon,
But Wilkinson is as sly as any fox.
He wants to grasp the honors for himself.
Jefferson has given him excuse —
How can I force him to ignite the match?
Then England would respond with ships and coin.
Jefferson will grasp at any straw
To ruin me if I make one false step.
This is my last and only chance to rise
And gain my rightful place in this brief life.

Why is it that I must always fight alone?
What was it Uncle Timothy once said —
My "tendency to go to grave extremes
Caused by insanity within my blood!"
Well, how can I help being what I am?
To serve my country's interests is my aim.
Is that insanity? Is that extreme?
When I have conquered Spanish Mexico
And added it to these United States,
I will have then surpassed Napoleon's feat!
The world and Jefferson will sing my praise.
Texas, Mexico and California
Should all be parts of these United States!
If only Jefferson might understand
And trust me to obtain this longed-for end,
My name would shine throughout all history
And my ambition then would be achieved!
Now is the time to act. I cannot wait!
Wilkinson and Jackson have the power,
And I the brains, to consummate this coup.
If only Wilkinson will play the game!
Perhaps I've erred in trusting him too far,
Who knows? I can't go back! I must go on!

[*He turns again to the letter he has been writing to
Theo, when a faint sound is heard at the gate. Now
he turns his eyes towards the noise, rises and grasps
the table, thinking he must be dreaming for there
coming through the gate is an apparition — or is it
really Theo in the flesh? He staggers forward and
they clasp each other in their arms.*]

AARON:

Can this be true? Have you really come at last?

THEO [*Kissing him and clinging to him*]:
Yes, I'm here. It's not an apparition!
We're at the Inn — Joseph and Gampy and I —
I hoped to find you all alone, so I walked here.

116

[*She is 25, looks emaciated, seems frustrated, but carries her head high. She is dressed in a neatly fitting blue frock.*]

I could die of happiness! Let us sit down.

AARON:
But what of me? This is my highest moment.
I'd given you up! I have stayed too long,
Hoping for a letter every day!
Now, you've come! Thank God you arrived in time,
For I must leave at sunrise. Such is fate!
Everything depends upon prompt action!

THEO:
What a time we've had! The roads are terrible.
Joseph complaining, your little grandson vomiting,
And I a nervous wreck for fear I'd miss you!
Now tell me all! You look just like a ghost!

AARON:
I'll make it brief, for I must see my grandson!
Jackson is my devoted friend. I trust him.
I've written you about my difficulties.
I've not completed this — please read it later.

[*Handing her his unfinished letter which she puts in her purse.*]

My projects all depend on Wilkinson.
I dare not trust him! All the West would rise
And follow me in driving out the Spaniards.
I dare not move until war is declared!
I think Wilkinson wants to head the movement
And that he is holding Jefferson back —
But he professes loyalty to me!
In ninety days my fate will be decided!

THEO [*Showing distress and nervousness*]:
Shall we stay at the Inn instead of here?
Since you must leave, I think the Inn is best.

117

AARON:

Yes, my darling, we could have more privacy —
We have so much to tell each other!
Now let me see you smile. You must not suffer
For my misfortunes. You're my pride and joy.

[*Patting her shoulder.*]

THEO:

Surely General Wilkinson will do what you want!
But I see fear and doubt within your eyes!
You're hounded just because you're fearless!
Surely God will save you from these dreadful men.
They're wicked and self-seeking. You're good!

[*Clinging to him in tears.*]

AARON:

Stop this! You are a woman of the world.
We must take life just as it comes. Dry your tears!
If I can now act quickly, I will win!
The whole country is ready for war —
Jackson, the British ships, the Creoles —
But Wilkinson's duplicity could ruin me!
I must forestall him. That's the picture!
Come now, let us find Mrs. Jackson,
And then I'll see my grandson at the Inn.

[*They walk to the door of the mansion house and
enter, Aaron's arm around Theodosia. It is noon and
the sun is high in the sky. They walk briskly and
seem like happy young lovers reunited. As they dis-
appear, Wilkinson comes from the gate and stealthily
walks to the table and picks up an envelope Aaron
had left there. He opens the flap and, showing dis-
appointment, throws it back on the table.*]

WILKINSON [*Mutters in an angry voice*]:
Empty, but it makes no difference; I heard him.
He is suspicious and would forestall me.
I defy him! But I must be more cautious!
I shall be patient and act at the right time.

118

I shall find a way to convince Jackson
Of his treasonable designs. Jefferson already knows.
So, proceed Colonel Burr in your own way!
I shall catch you red-handed and with evidence!
A court martial will end your crafty career!
I know Thomas Jefferson will richly reward me!

CURTAIN

## ACT THREE

### SCENE THREE

SCENE: *Bayou Pierre, a thriving river town on the Mississippi, in the Territory of Louisiana, January 20, 1807. A bay extending from the Mississippi, thirty miles above Natchez. The afternoon sun is shining and the water sparkling in the bay like diamonds. The live oaks and low-growing shrubs on the bank give a beautiful green frame to a nature picture, and the water reflects trees and clouds which extend far away into the distance. Nine staunch river boats — batteaux — are anchored in a group in the bay with native fishing vessels interspersed. It is the widely-heralded military fleet of Aaron Burr. The largest of the boats is tied up at the rustic wharf in the center at the back of the stage. It is Aaron's flagship.*

*On the right is a flat, sandy beach with a number of skiffs hauled up above high water. A huge trunk of a dead tree is lying in the sand with four young men seated on it — each dressed in homespun.*

*On the left is the village — its houses painted on the screen and extending into the distance, with the side of one particular house near the wharf open and oc-*

119

*cupying about one-fifth of the stage. It is Judge
Bruin's law office — two desks, chairs, matting-cov-
ered floor, with maps hanging on the walls, and a
door on the left.*

*Aaron Burr is seated at one of the desks and is read-
ing a newspaper. He looks careworn and bewildered.
Outside, the boys seated on the log strike up a conversation.*

FIRST BOY:
They say that he intends to give himself up.

SECOND BOY:
He'll find a way to clear himself as always.
Why do they keep on hounding him this way?
He has not committed any crime!
No jury will indict him; that has been proved.

THIRD BOY:
We have had a wonderful time since joining him.
That week on Blennerhassett Island has fitted us
For war or for Washita — I care not which!

FOURTH BOY:
I think he has given up hope that war will come.
He is assembling us to tell the facts.

[*During this conversation, skiffs loaded with boys
are approaching the beach from the moored boats.
They are gathering around in a group on the right.
On the left of the stage, a small clean-shaven man enters the law office and shakes Aaron's hand. He is
dressed in a black cloth tailcoat with ruffled shirt and
cuffs and high collar. He wears black knee breeches,
white stockings and black low shoes. It is Judge
Bruin, who now takes the chair near Aaron, and
looks at him with piercing black eyes but with kindness and pathos.*]

JUDGE BRUIN:
I see that you are reading that damned article

120

Which quotes your letter to General Wilkinson,
In which you say you have the men and funds,
And will not wait for war to be declared.

AARON [*Rising and walking about in anger*]:

Yes, but these are not the words I wrote him.
He is making me out a traitor and a rebel,
Stirring up the West against the East.
This is a plain forgery. He must be mad!

BRUIN:
That is why I sent for you. Look at these!

[*Showing him a stack of newspapers.*]

They all contain the stories of your rebellion.
Wilkinson has been playing a double game.
The whole country is convinced of your treason.

AARON:
I can prove that he is a fraud and liar!

BRUIN:
How can you do that except by court action?
Jefferson trusts him. How can you apprehend him?
He has also fooled Jackson and Adair.
He has been in the pay of Spain all along,
And was at the time of your Nashville conference.

AARON [*With white face and hands trembling*]:
I can't believe it! I am overcome!
How did you find it out? I've been a fool!

BRUIN:
General Adair secured proof from a friend.
I've sent for him, too. He should be here now.

AARON:
I only know, from reading the papers,
That I've been cruelly misrepresented.
The people in the East have come to think
That I'm a villian, stirring up rebellion.
My friends all know I have no such designs.

121

BRUIN:

Those nine small boats now anchored in the bay
Could not transport 2,000 well-trained troops
To siege New Orleans, as Wilkinson proclaims.
Jefferson, I'm told, believes this nonsense.
Spain has settled all her differences with us.
The newspapers all say your presence in New Orleans
Is intended to start a Creole uprising.

AARON:

How perfectly ridiculous! Here's the list.

[*Taking a paper from his pocket.*]

Just sixty raw recruits prepared for farming —
Or for war, if war had been declared.
We know, at length, the latter is a dream.
I've called a meeting for this afternoon,
To systematize the staking off of claims.
The Washita project is our only hope.

BRUIN:

Aaron, there is no hope! Where have you been
That you are so uninformed about the facts?

AARON:

I secured three boats, Blennerhassett three,
And Comfort Tyler four, at Marietta.
We came together December Thirty-first.
We've kept in hiding, avoiding cities.
My scouts, Swartwout and Bollman, will meet me
here
In your hospitable office — that was the plan.
My next move all depends on their reports.

BRUIN:

Now let me tell you what you do not know.
New Orleans is under martial law.
Its citizens are in a state of terror.

[*Picking up one of the newspapers.*]

Here is a paragraph from the *Western Spy* —

122

A fair example of all other papers:
"Colonel Burr has built great ships of war at Wheel-
    ing,
Also Marietta. He has collected
Vast quantities of naval equipment
At Lewisville, prepared to seize New Orleans."

AARON:

That is perfectly preposterous! Ridiculous!
They are all determined to ruin me!

BRUIN:

You have not heard it all. Five legislatures
Have recently passed laws, all aimed at you,
To stave off war-like enterprises.
The President has ordered your arrest.
He has also issued a proclamation,
Requesting loyal citizens to withdraw
From your unlawful enterprises.

AARON:

To think that Jefferson should stoop so low!
His only evidence based on vicious lies
From newspapers, inspired by Wilkinson,
Who wants to head the expedition himself!
I defy them all! The truth will prevail!

BRUIN:

Don't be too sure about the truth prevailing.
History may paint you as committing treason.

[*Picking up another paper.*]

This is from the *Lexington Gazette*:
"Our opinion of Colonel Burr has been reversed
By the President's recent communication
To Congress, and by General Eaton's statement."

AARON:

What was his statement? I thought he was my friend!

123

BRUIN:

    I'm amazed you have not seen the newspapers!
    He said that you had told him of your project
    To revolutionize the territory
    West of the Alleghenys, and establish
    An empire, with New Orleans the capital,
    Then carry the conquest into Mexico.

AARON:

    How could a war hero indulge in slander!

BRUIN:

    Your friends know you are innocent, but I fear
    The public always likes to think the worst.

AARON:

    I will fight this calumny unto the end.
    No honest jury would ever find me guilty.

BRUIN:

    Your trial will never be before a jury.
    If Wilkinson can have you court martialed,
    My friend, you will not have the slightest chance!

AARON [*Turning pale and pacing the floor*]:

    Of course, you're right. They have me in a trap!

BRUIN:

    I say, disappear before they handcuff you
    And take you to New Orleans for speedy trial.
    Their verdict will be death before a firing squad!

AARON:

    My God! and this from you, an honored judge
    And my dear friend! Of course, I can't do that!
    I never run away when I am accused!

BRUIN:

    Wait a minute! You have always done just that.
    You ran away from your Uncle Timothy!
    You came West to escape a murder trial!
    Now you must escape at once to save your life!

124

AARON:

But, I'd be a fugitive with a price offered
For my capture, dead or alive, just like a beast.

BRUIN:

Well, let us wait! Adair should soon be here.
But remember, you're a marked and hunted man,
Run down by the President of the U. S.,
Who's backed by ninety per cent of the people,
All of whom believe in his integrity.
They do not stop to think he might be wrong.

AARON:

But where could I go? It is not feasible!
I'll surrender and take my chances.
It is all hearsay, trumped-up evidence,
Inspired by Wilkinson. What wrong have I commit-
    ted?
The whole country expected war with Spain
When they crossed the line and shot down our flag.
I was ready for it — that's the trouble!
I never thought of leading a rebellion.
Has Jefferson refrained from war, just to spite me?

BRUIN:

Perhaps he did not want you as the leader!

AARON:

We are bound eventually to annex
Texas and California. By acting now
We could include Mexico — do you agree?

[At this moment there is a loud knock on the door.
Judge Bruin hastens to open it and two men enter.
They are Dr. Eric Bollman, the famous German-
American who attempted to rescue Lafayette — a
tall, distinguished man of 38, with keen blue eyes
and powdered wig and one of Aaron Burr's great
friends and followers — and General Adair, now in
citizen's clothing. They show much excitement as
they shake hands and exchange salutations and then
take chairs.]

125

BRUIN [*Looking at the newcomers*]:
  Thank God you have arrived, and just in time.

AARON:
  My friends, I'm in a quandary. Tell me all —
  And I suggest that Eric should speak first.

DR. BOLLMAN:
  Very well, since you desire it, I shall begin.
  I was promptly seized by orders from Wilkinson.
  When found not guilty, I went at once to Jefferson
  To try to break down all his prejudice.
  I told him I had come of my free will,
  Attempting to remove the false impression
  That he had formed of my friend, Aaron Burr.
  I said the newspaper statements were not true,
  That there was nothing treasonable about you.
  I urged him to declare a war on Spain
  As a patriotic duty craved by all,
  And put you at the head of the adventure.
  He listened patiently and seemed my friend.
  He complimented me on my attempt
  To rescue Lafayette from Austrian prisons.
  Imagine my surprise to get a letter
  It would be improper to keep still!
  I refused it as a badge of infamy —
  As though I were a culprit or a felon!
  When party spite and passion go that far
  It would be improper to keep still!
  That is why I've come to warn you. I advise
  To try to get away while there is time!
  A court martial trial would surely mean your death.

  [*He turns inquiring eyes on Aaron, who rises and
  puts his hand affectionately on Bollman's shoulder.*]

AARON:
  Your obligation to a sense of justice
  Has forced you on the natural path of duty.
  As sure as there's a God, He will reward you
  For what you've done to help the cause of justice!

126

*[Then turning to Adair.]*

Now let us hear from General Adair, a victim
Of this administration's poisoned darts.

ADAIR:

Little did I think at Andrew Jackson's
That I'd be made to suffer pangs of torture.
Wilkinson is a villain, dyed in Satan's fat!
You'll remember it was planned that I should go
To New Orleans to help prepare for you.
I found fair lodging; sent a note at once
To Wilkinson announcing that I'd arrived —
I notified the Governor as well —
And I called upon the Catholic Bishop.
He was enthusiastic about our plan
To conquer Mexico. But then he paused
And showed a letter signed by Patrick Mangan,
Rector of the College of Salamanka,
Requesting, on the part of Wilkinson,
The payment of Two hundred thousand dollars
To partly compensate for warding off
The invasion of Mexico by Aaron Burr!
It is a fact! I saw it with my own eyes.

AARON:

Such perfidy! He is a Judas! A cur!

ADAIR:

I then decided to leave the city at once.
I saw that it was in an utter panic.
The streets were barricaded and soldiers drilling!
Placards on the public buildings everywhere,
Containing extracts from your private letters
And, of course, the President's proclamation!

AARON:

How can that arch-fiend dare to do such things?

BRUIN:

He dares because the President is behind him!

127

ADAIR:

    Arriving at my boarding house, I found
    A Colonel Kingsbury with a troop of soldiers.
    I was paraded through the streets, a culprit!
    I was denied the writ of habeas corpus!

AARON:

    It is beyond belief! What are we coming to?

ADAIR:

    Then I was tried at Baltimore by Judge Nicholson,
    Along with Ogden and your friend, Swartwout.
    We were released for lack of any proof.
    On hearing this, the President remarked,
    "Their crimes have been defeated. Their punishment
    Belongs to quite a different department."

AARON:

    That shows he is vindictive and unfair.

ADAIR:

    It proves, Aaron, that you have not a chance.
    My advice to you is, leave this country at once.

AARON [*Showing reluctance*]:

    But that, I think, is going much too far.
    Heretofore, I've faced their vicious charges!
    They have no proof that I've committed a crime!
    Therefore, I want to face them without fear.

BOLLMAN:

    My friend, you talk just like a little child.
    I urge you now to go while there is time.

BRUIN:

    So my advice is backed by these, your friends!
    We love you and would save you if we can.

AARON:

    The fate of men and nations hangs on threads.
    Canada we lost by lack of snow!
    Shall we lose Mexico through one man's spite?

128

[*At this moment, Samuel Swartwout and Ogden burst into the room. They are in boots and spurs and covered with dust — showing a long journey.*]

AARON [*Showing excitement as he shakes hands*]:
My friends, you've come at the critical hour.
My future plans depend on your advice.

SWARTWOUT:
Thank God, we've come in time to save your life.
Three hundred militiamen are on their way
To seize your boats, your officers and you —
And turn you over to Wilkinson's court martial!
They will shoot you down unless you can escape.

AARON [*Putting his arms around the shoulders of Swartwout and Ogden*]:

You have brought my indecision to an end.
I will undertake escape at your advice.

OGDEN:
It's the only thing to do to save your life.

BRUIN:
We're losing time. You must be off at once!

AARON:
But when this storm blows over, I shall return,
With aid from Europe. I then shall force a war.
This northern continent must be united.
My life's ambition yet will be fulfilled!

BRUIN:
Time will decide all that. Meantime, be quick!

AARON:
I must see Blennerhassett and Comfort Tyler,
And speak to those brave boys who wait out there.
I ordered them to come to hear my plans
For going a hundred miles to the Washita.
It is a tragic ending of my dreams!
But I'm not through. Someday, I shall return!

129

*[Then turning to Judge Bruin.]*

Judge Bruin, can you find a horse and guide?

*[He shakes hands with all his devoted friends and rushes through the door to the beach, where his recruits are gathered in groups. They all stand up and cheer as he approaches them. Aaron braces himself for the ordeal — with Bollman, Ogden and Adair at his side.]*

AARON:
My dear friends, when I asked you to assemble
I did not know a sudden turn of fate
Would alter my remarks. I had intended
To say the longed-for declaration of war
On which our Mexican adventure depended
Was now a hope deferred, and that, therefore,
I would lead you to the Washita Lands,
Whose fertile acres await development.
Now, however, you must be content
With other leaders, as my path is blocked.
Harman Blennerhassett and Comfort Tyler,
I would select, but they must now decide!

*[A loud murmur runs through the crowd. Blennerhassett turns toward Aaron in excitement. He raises his hand to silence the murmurs so that he can be heard.]*

BLENNERHASSETT *[Looking directly at Aaron]*:
What does this mean? We've blindly followed you!
Just what has happened to impede our course?
We've all become suspicious of your plans
Since you continued down the Mississippi!
If you were taking us to those farm lands,
Why did you not stop at the nearest point?

AARON *[Showing distress]*:
We came here to find out the latest facts.
These, my friends, are my scouts to find the truth.
It is on their advice that I am acting.

130

When I have finished, they will tell you all.
Just let me say, my enemies have won!
They have convinced the willing President
That I am leading a rebellion of the West
Against the United States. This is no news!
You all know I've been tried three times for this.
No jury would convict me. I've gone free.
But now it's different! General Wilkinson
Has sent three hundred militiamen
To conduct me as a prisoner to New Orleans
And hand me to a military court
Which will not fail to shoot me dead for treason!

Therefore, within this hour I have decided
To go to France till reason is restored.
I am appointing Mister Blennerhassett
To equally distribute all my wealth
Among you who have been my trusted friends —
Including these batteaux, which will be sold.
You're free to do whatever you think best.
The Washita Land is yours to cultivate —
Though some of you may want to go back home.
It breaks my heart to say good-bye and leave you,
But God knows that my conscience still is clear.
I must depart at once or I'll be seized!

[*Then turning to Blennerhassett and handing him
his keys, and with a trembling voice.*]

To Harman Blennerhassett I present
These keys to both my chests in yonder boat.

[*He points to his flagship, tied up at the wharf, then
turns to Adair.*]

General Adair, will you now please take charge
And tell these friends of mine all further facts.

[*A loud murmur of protest is heard as Aaron turns
and dashes into Judge Bruin's office and bolts the
door. The boys on the beach all crowd around General Adair and his two companions. All are asking*

131

*questions at once, drowning out Adair's voice. Pandemonium takes place as he tries to address the crowd. Some are seen pointing to a gunboat which is approaching at high speed up the river. All is excitement and confusion.*

*While this is taking place on the outside, Aaron is seen in Judge Bruin's office, hastily exchanging his homespun clothing and boots for an old blanket coat with a leather strap holding it in place around his waist, to which a tin cup is suspended on the left and a scalping knife on the right. Judge Bruin hands him a battered white felt hat and pair of muddy boots with spurs, which Aaron quickly puts on.]*

BRUIN [*In a stealthy, excited voice and looking at Aaron with compassion*]:

Outside this door you'll find a splendid horse.
Colonel Osmun, my neighbor, has provided it.
Chester Ashley, a reliable guide and friend,
Is mounted, ready to accompany you.
He'll escort you through the jungle wilds
And past the hostile Indian villages.
At Pensacola, there's a British ship.
I hope you can with safety get aboard.

AARON [*Now in perfect disguise, puts his hand on Judge Bruin's shoulder affectionately*]:
God bless you! This may be my only chance!

BRUIN:
Wait! The *New Orleans Picayune* has come!

[*He holds up the paper and reads aloud from the front page.*]

"Two thousand dollars reward for the capture
Of Aaron Burr, former Vice President."
This seems to prove your friends' advice is sound.

AARON [*With anger and disgust, glances at the paper, as he dashes through the door*]:

132

You are right! I must risk my chances.

[*On the outside, while Aaron is preparing to escape, the gunboat approaches the shore. The boys continue their debate about what to do, which is silenced as the militiamen come ashore and surround them with pointed guns and flashing sabers.*]

CAPTAIN SCOTT [*Of the militia*]:
Anyone who attempts to escape will be shot!
I arrest you all in the name of the law,
And by order of the Governor of Mississippi.

[*Blennerhassett, Tyler, Adair, Bollman and Ogden are handcuffed and taken in a small boat, under guard, to the gunboat, which is anchored near the shore. The militiamen board and seize the nine river boats. The boys are herded in groups, excitedly discussing their fate.*]

CAPTAIN SCOTT:
Are there any officers among you?

[*The boys are silent. No one moves.*]

If not, you are free to go your own ways.
I have executed my orders. Now go!

CURTAIN

# ACT THREE

## SCENE FOUR

SCENE: *Penetentiary, Richmond. Aaron Burr's sumptuous quarters on the top floor of the Penetentiary in Richmond, Virginia, July 30, 1807. It is a sunny day and the room is glistening with light. The room occupies the whole stage and presents the appearance*

133

*of a gentleman's house — net curtains on the windows*
*with draperies of red damask, a gray Brussels carpet,*
*two large divans upholstered in black mohair, a che-*
*val glass and three oil paintings hanging on the wall*
*— one over the marble mantel; several side chairs are*
*arranged about the room. There are two large ma-*
*hogany doors — one at each end of the room — and*
*two large windows, at one of which Theodosia Alston*
*is standing, pensively gazing out. She is dressed in a*
*light green chiffon costume with puffed sleeves and*
*a high bust and slim waist. She is bareheaded; her*
*hair is a beautiful auburn. A lace veil is draped*
*over a Grecian knot. She has a firm mouth and large,*
*piercing hazel eyes. She murmurs to herself aloud.*

THEODOSIA:
So this has been my father's habitation
For four long months of dire uncertainty.
How he maintains his calm and pleasant mien
Is something I can never understand.
To think this is a penitentiary,
With bedrooms, dining room and service
Where he can visit with his friends!
All men and women of the social set
Flock here by the score to entertain him.

To be indicted for misdemeanor
Is humiliating, but for treason, too,
Makes my heart ache with terror's fearful pangs.
He would not let me come to him till now.
I think I should have been here all the time
To comfort him and cheer him with my love.
My room, in what he calls his mansion,
Is comfortable and cozy beyond belief,
But when I think this is my father's prison,
To hold him fast until he comes to trial,
I feel despair which I disguise by smiles.
He must not learn that Joseph turns his back
For fear that he, too, might become involved.
This visit is the acme of my life.

134

My life or death, as well as Aaron Burr's,
Depends upon the verdict of the court!

[*The door on the right opens and Aaron enters the
room with quick steps and a sprightly smile. He is
dressed immaculately in a dark purple, long-tailed
coat, knee britches with white stockings, black shoes
with silver buckles; white silk waistcoat with ruffled
front cuffs, tall soft white collar and a black, well-
groomed wig. He rushes over to the window where
Theo is standing.*]

AARON:
Why are you so engrossed, my darling child?

THEO [*As they embrace and stand together at the win-
dow*]:
I've been looking at the lines of carriages,
The shining hats of all the Negro coachmen —
Quite different from our quiet country place.
I wish I had come here long weeks ago.

[*On the verge of tears.*]

AARON:
Tut, tut, now! None of that! You tried to come,
But I would not permit it, as you know.
I thought the jury never would indict me,
Since I am to be tried, it is quite different.
I wanted you as a witness by my side
To judge my conduct and the government's.

THEO:
It is too terrible! When will it start?

AARON:
As soon as they can find twelve honest men.
They have already been two weeks at it.
It seems that everyone has taken sides.
It won't be long. Meantime, your presence here
In Richmond and your presence in my "mansion"
Has produced a definite impression
Everywhere — and I'm a happier man.

135

THEO:
And certainly I am a happier woman.

AARON:
Our letters kept us posted as to facts,
But ten days for transmission changed the scene.

[*A Negro attendant enters the room and hands a
note to Theo, who rapidly reads it and turns to her
father.*]

THEO:
Your friend, Mrs. Wickham, called in her barouche
To show the town to Joseph and your grandson.
She said she knew that I would not leave you.

AARON:
Kind of her! Now we can talk in peace.

THEO:
Begin with your escape from Bayou Pierre —
A terrible experience, I know.
A sudden change when all was going well!

AARON:
I wrote you all the details every week.

THEO:
I want to hear it from your very lips.

AARON:
When I heard that they had gone to the extent
Of offering a reward for my arrest,
I knew I'd made a serious mistake.
To turn back then, I felt, would be too late.
Judge Bruin's guide had left me with a map
Which showed the trails to Pensacola Town.
For two weeks all went well. I begged for food.
At nights I slept in barns with my faithful horse.
I felt secure until I reached Wakefield,
And stopped to ask my way and show my map.
A frontier lawyer, Nicholas Perkins,

136

Said that he thought that I was Aaron Burr!
He notified the court and claimed the reward.
I was surrounded by a troop of cavalry.

THEO:

You poor darling! You did not write me that.

AARON:

We stopped in a small South Carolina town.
I sprang from off my horse and called to a group
Nearby and said that I was Aaron Burr,
To rescue me from this illegal arrest!
But no one moved! They forced me on my horse —
My most humiliating experience!
Now let us talk about more cheerful things.
Tell me in detail all about yourself.

THEO [*Carried away by emotion and sympathy*]:

I want to hear the rest. Please tell me all.

AARON:

I was kept at Fort Stoddard for two weeks.
I made a host of friends and, when I left,
They gave me an ovation, waving flags!
Now I have been here four long months. Why? Why?

THEO:

But, father dear, you have been lionized!

AARON:

It matters not, since Jefferson has power!
He hates me and he wants to see me hanged.
He's brought great pressure on Chief Justice
      Marshall.

THEO:

How can that be? How does he dare do that?

AARON:

Let me tell you what happened to my friends.
Ogden, Adair, poor Bollman and Swartwout
Were tried for treason and declared not guilty.
Wilkinson had tried to have them sentenced
Just because they were loyal friends.

137

THEO:
> What has happened to Mister Blennerhassett
> And Margaret, his beautiful and gracious wife?
> Did that most dreadful mob destroy their island?

AARON:
> Yes, they burnt his house and every building.
> The hapless fellow is now awaiting trial.
> The worst of it is he now has turned on me,
> Suspicious because I passed on down the river
> Instead of stopping at the nearest point
> To the Washita Lands. I did not know
> At that time of the treachery of Wilkinson!

THEO:
> Do you blame it all on General Wilkinson?

AARON:
> Yes, chiefly so, but sly old Jefferson
> Was looking for excuse to ruin me.
> His proclamation turned most all the papers
> To enemies, which formerly were my friends,
> Not realizing that he had no proof
> To support the vicious charges he made.

THEO:
> Why did the General do these things to you?

AARON:
> To save himself! He is despicable!
> Let me read this letter from John Randolph.
> I brought it for your husband and for you,
> As evidence from an unprejudiced source —
> For no man can deny John Randolph's honesty:
> "Wilkinson is from bark to core a villain!
> I never saw man's nature so degraded!
> And yet he holds executive prestige.
> I know for years he's been employed by Spain."

THEO:
> Why, Father dear, did you trust such a man?

138

AARON:

I often ask myself that very question.
We were comrades at Quebec, that is all.
When he came back into my life I fell
Into his trap. It was my greatest error.

THEO:

Father, I think you are superlative!
I know you will go free in this long trial.

AARON:

It all depends on Wilkinson's testimony.
Can I or can I not break it all down?
To think the President recommended him
To Congress as deserving gratitude
As a worthy citizen and gallant soldier
To me is too revolting to be decent!

THEO:

I agree, but tell me more about yourself.

AARON:

My poor recruits were all at once arrested,
But later freed and turned loose on their own,
To forage as farmers, teachers and what not!
I suffer mental anguish about their fate.
I hope that someday I may rescue them.

THEO:

Poor darling! They'll understand you and forgive!
They'd be surprised to see your prison here.

AARON:

I'm sure you're right! My wonderful attorneys
Visit me constantly, and all the elite
Of Richmond have showered me with kindness.
They have provided a lovely house for you,
Your husband and your son, one block away.
You know you are to move to it tomorrow.
They have provided most efficient slaves.
It is fantastic that they honor me!

139

THEO:

It seems that I am living in a dream,
And not real life. I am so very happy
To find you in good health and confident.
I shall go now and bring you your namesake.

[*She leaves the room, Aaron looking after her with
anxiety. He then mutters to himself.*]

AARON:

Little Theo is almost broken-hearted
Over my incarceration and my trial.
If I'm found guilty it will cause her death.
I'll do my best and keep on smiling.
She shall be proud of me! I must be cleared!
I have nothing to fear since I am innocent.

## CURTAIN

# ACT FOUR

## SCENE ONE

SCENE: *Trial for treason. The Virginia House of Burgesses, September 1, 1807. A large gloomy room filled on the right and left with a conglomerate mass of men representing the melting pot of Democracy — the painted screen carrying the crowd into the distance. Everyone for miles around who could fight his way to the makeshift courtroom is present to see the former Vice President of the United States on trial for his life. It is one of the high spots in the history of America. A contest between Thomas Jefferson and John Marshall, between throne and bench. Chief Justice Marshall in his black robe is on the bench at the center and rear of the stage. Calm, deliberate and fearless, he is a tall, slender man of fifty-two, with a majestic head, large brilliant brown eyes — only to be matched by the superb ones of Aaron Burr! Colonel Burr, immaculately dressed in black silk*

141

*small-clothes, with ruffled white shirt and stock, is*
*at the table on the right, and is surrounded by the*
*most brilliant corps of lawyers ever assembled in*
*America. They are Edmund Randolph, who had*
*been a delegate to the Philadelphia Convention and*
*also Secretary of State in Washington's Cabinet; John*
*Wickham, ablest lawyer in Richmond; Benjamin*
*Botts, keen-witted and aggressive, who ranks as a close*
*second; Jack Baker, very brilliant; Charlie Lee, late*
*Attorney General; and Luther Martin of Maryland,*
*who enjoys the reputation of having the greatest legal*
*talents of the day.*

*The government is represented by District Attorney*
*George Hay, Associate Counsel William Wirt and*
*Alexander McRae. In the jury box, Colonel Carring-*
*ton, foreman of the jury, is conspicuous for his*
*benign facial expression. He is surrounded by the*
*other eleven men, all alert, and some bending for-*
*ward in eagerness, not to miss one word. Tension*
*is noted on the faces and in the attitudes of everyone*
*in the room.*

*Colonel Burr is in whispered conversation with his*
*chief counsel, Luther Martin, an ungainly, huge,*
*bloated-faced individual with unsteady legs and*
*husky voice. Martin rises and addresses the court.*

MARTIN:
Your Honor, this trial has dragged on for four weeks,
And we have examined fifty witnesses —
I think thirty of them have prejured themselves;
But we can bring it to an early close
If you will subpoena the President.
We want him on the witness stand not only
Because he plays the role of prosecutor,
Trying to hound my client to the gibbet
Through animosity and prejudice,
But because he possesses a certain letter
Written by our client to General Wilkinson.

142

The accused should have this letter in defense
As vital, necessary evidence.
The President has also undertaken
To prejudice my client by declaring
To the world that "of his guilt there is no doubt."
He assumes the knowledge of Almighty God
To judge the heart of my respected friend.
His sense of justice has become so warped
That he has gone to the extreme extent
Of suggesting that I should also be included
With my client in the charge of treason.

AARON:

Your Honor, our President is a gifted lawyer.
He certainly should know just what war is.
He proclaimed there was one six long months ago.
They have been hunting for it ever since,
But cannot find it — except in newspapers.
We need him here to tell us where it is.

[*Loud laughter is heard from all parts of the closely-
packed courtroom. At a nod from the Chief Justice,
the marshal raps with his gavel for order. Silence is
at last obtained.*]

CHIEF JUSTICE MARSHALL:

As you well know, the President refused
To honor the subpoena that I served,
On grounds that then appealed to me as proper —
And I am still convinced that I am right.
The leading feature of our Constitution
Is the independence of its three branches,
The Legislative, the Executive,
And the Judiciary — each one distinct.
A subpoena of our country's President
Is therefore unconstitutional.
The objection is accordingly sustained.

MARTIN:

Your Honor, you are making history.
But we are not interested in history,
But only in clearing our client from guilt.

143

THE CHIEF JUSTICE:
  The simple fact to prove in this case
  Is the assembling of force for levying war —
  A completely visible transaction,
  Plainly witnessed by a number of people.
  Months have elapsed since its alleged occurrence.
  If it occurred, why has it not been proved?

MARTIN:
  Your Honor, that is what we want to know.
  The President has made the greatest effort.
  I have before me here his very words:

  [Reading from paper.]

  "We have set on foot an urgent enquiry
  Throughout the whole of the United States,
  No expense to be spared, to get witnesses
  Who will satisfy the world if not the court,
  Of the unquestioned guilt of Colonel Burr."

HAY [Rising and addressing the chair]:
  Your Honor, what is the objective here?

MARTIN:
  Your Honor, it is to present a fact.
  Our client is handicapped by lack of funds.
  The government admits twelve thousand dollars
  For witnesses thus far. If Colonel Burr
  Had the means, he could bring witnesses to court
  Not alone to foil his prosecutors,
  But to render them each one ridiculous.
  We're giving him our services gratis,
  And only because we still believe in justice.

THE CHIEF JUSTICE:
  Let us proceed with other witnesses.

HAY:
  Your Honor, we will put upon the stand
  General William Eaton of the U. S. Army.
  We hope to prove through him the act of treason.

144

*[A tall, rough-looking man wearing a red Turkish sash, commemorating his feats in Africa, is conducted to the witness stand and given the oath.]*

General, do you know the defendant — and how long?

EATON:
I have known him well for a long, long time.

HAY:
Tell the jury the offer that he made you
To help him revolutionize the West.

EATON [*Taking an aggressive attitude*]:
He offered me a dignified command
In the army, and laid open his project
To establish an extensive new empire
West of the Alleghenys — himself as chief!
Also to organize a fighting force
On the Mississippi, to seize all Mexico!
He said, if I would join in this conspiracy,
He'd collect my claim against the government,
And also pay me a large indemnity.

HAY:
Was this payment included in his plan?

EATON:
Yes, he repeated it to me three times.

AARON:
You spoke of claims against the government.
Were they ever paid? How much did you receive?

EATON [*Addressing the court*]:
Your Honor, is that a proper question?

AARON:
Your Honor, I want to prove the vicious bias
That exists within the mind of this witness.

THE CHIEF JUSTICE [*Addressing the witness*]:
Yes! You may answer Colonel Burr's question.

EATON:

Ten thousand dollars! But that is my affair.

AARON:

When was all that money received by you —
No doubt by order of the President!

EATON:

Last March. But that is only my concern!

AARON:

Was it just before or just after the date
Of my arrest and my arraignment for treason?

EATON:

I don't remember. It does not concern you!

[*Laughter echoes through the courtroom. Booing
is heard from some quarters. Justice Marshall uses
his gavel and looks with vexation on the disturbers.*]

HAY:

We have no further questions for this witness.

[*Eaton is conducted from the room by the marshal,
who brings in another witness. The clerk announces
his name, Jacob Albright, and at a nod from the
Chief Justice, administers the oath.*]

Your Honor, we hope to prove by this witness
That the overt act of war was committed.
Mister Albright, tell this patient jury
In what capacity you were employed
On Blennerhassett and what you observed.

ALBRIGHT:

I was hired to build a kiln on the island
For drying corn. About December tenth,
I saw the boatmen running many bullets.
I heard one say, "Let's run more bullets —
As many as we can fire! Let's say twelve rounds!"
Then a man called Tupper came along
And laid his hands on Blennerhassett.

146

I heard him say, "You now are in my hands,
In the name of the law!" Then the boys sprang up,
And leveled their muskets at poor Tupper's head.
He let loose of Mister Blennerhassett at once!

HAY:
How many armed men do you think were there?

ALBRIGHT:
I would say about twenty or thirty.

AARON:
Was it General Tupper of Marietta?

ALBRIGHT:
Yes, that's the name. He lives in Marietta.

AARON:
Your Honor, since Blennerhassett's Island
Is in Virginia, I think General Tupper
Had no legal right to make an arrest.
The act of resisting an illegal seizure
Is considered only self-defense, not treason.
I ask therefore that this man's testimony
Be eliminated from the evidence.

THE CHIEF JUSTICE:
The request is granted. Now let us proceed.

HAY:
Your Honor, we shall now present Peter Taylor.

[*Taylor takes his place and is sworn in, while Aaron
whispers to several of his counsel.*]

HAY:
Mister Taylor, what were your island duties,
And did you ever see Colonel Burr on the island?

TAYLOR:
I was Mister Blennerhassett's gardener.
I often saw Colonel Burr there on the island.
Mister Blennerhassett told me himself

147

That they were about to take all Mexico,
And that Colonel Burr was to become the king.
I asked him what would happen to the men
Who were to settle the lands they talked about.
He said, "Peter, by God, I'll stab any man
Who dares not to conform to all our orders."

HAY:

You mean Mister Blennerhassett is warlike,
And anxious to lead his men into Mexico?

TAYLOR:

Well, I could not go that far, Mister Hay.

[*Hay motions Aaron to take over, and sits down.*]

AARON:

You say you know Mister Blennerhassett well.
Would it not be ridiculous for him
To engage in any warlike enterprise?
About how far away can he distinguish
A man from a horse, with his very poor eyesight?

TAYLOR:

He could not know you at ten steps away.
He knows nothing of military matters,
But it was often mentioned by his people
That he had lots of sense, but no common sense.

[*Laughter throughout the courtroom.*]

HAY:

Thank you, Mister Taylor, you are excused.
Your Honor, I suggest one hour's recess.
We'll bring our final witness, General Wilkinson,
At one o'clock, if that meets your approval.

THE CHIEF JUSTICE:

I declare a recess of one hour.

[*He raps with his gavel and leaves the room. The
jury files out, also the visitors. Aaron remains at his
table talking to his attorneys. The latter soon depart,*]

*leaving him alone in the courtroom, making hasty notes. Theodosia suddenly returns to the room and rushes down the aisle and embraces her father.*]

THEODOSIA:
Father, I am sure you will be cleared.
How wonderful is this Chief Justice Marshall!
When you are free, I shall take you home with me.
You must have a rest after this ordeal.

AARON [*Rising and taking Theo's hand*]:
No, my dearest child, I cannot do that.
I want to go to Europe and collect
Money to reorganize my projects.
I may stay a year or more, and then join you.
If Jefferson dies, I shall return at once.
If he lives, I may return and face him
With the backing of England or France.

THEO:
Your tenacity of purpose is superb!

AARON:
Now go, darling, and kiss my grandson for me.
I must work on my plans for this afternoon.
They all depend upon Wilkinson.
I can shoot holes in his testimony.
I wish I could shoot one in his false heart.

THEO:
I shall do as you say. When will you sail?

AARON:
I shall take the very first ship I can catch.
I shall raise enough money in Philadelphia.
Joseph has invested enough in me;
I would not take another cent from him.

THEO:
You seem so confident! Might they convict you?

AARON:
That's impossible! I'll tell you the secret,

149

But never, please, divulge it to anyone.
Marshall hates old Jefferson! Now run along!
If possible join me after the verdict.
What a trial! Thirty days of foolishness!
Enough to turn one against our system!
I want to get away and cool off —
Perhaps talk to Napoleon! Who knows?
I'm thankful that you have good health and comforts.

[*They embrace and Theo rapidly departs. Aaron
returns to his seat and indulges in the habit of talking to himself.*]

If I'm convicted, Jefferson has won!
I will be promptly hanged — to this he's seen!
And he will ever gloat with selfish spleen,
Just as he did when I shot Hamilton!
If I am cleared, he'll hound me to my grave.
Why is it that man's hate exceeds his love?
The hand of fate swings downward from above —
Some lives to liquidate, some lives to save.
Predestination is my firm belief.
I've been the victim of a weird design.
By accident of chance I've missed my goal.
Some people look upon me as a thief.
My darling daughter thinks I am divine.
To keep her faith I would pay any toll.

This jury is intelligent and kind.
I think Chief Justice Marshall is my friend.
He knows that I'm not guilty of the charge,
But Hay is clever and may work some trick.
When Marshall granted me a jury trial,
I had a chance. A military court
Would certainly have had me shot at once.
I told my Theo that I had no fear.
It was to calm her. No one can be sure!
Jefferson and Marshall in a duel!
It is to laugh! Neither ever held a gun!

[*The sound of marching feet is heard. The jury files*

*in. The attorneys and those admitted to the court-room all take their places. The noise subsides. The marshal raises his voice as the Chief Justice reaches his chair.*]

THE MARSHAL:
Oyez! Oyez! The Honorable Court
Is now in session. Let all be seated!

[*He raps with his gavel and all is silence.*]

HAY:
Your Honor, the prosecution desires
To present General Wilkinson, its chief witness.

[*The general is conducted to the witness stand. He is in full uniform, and swaggers to his seat with the eyes of everyone in the room fixed on him, except those of Aaron and Martin, who are engaged in whispered conversation and ignore him. Wilkinson is in a parallel line with Aaron and looks like a turkey cock. He is plainly bracing himself for an encounter with Aaron's eyes. When Wilkinson's name is called and he takes the oath, Aaron turns his head and looks the general full in the face, with a piercing, contemptuous expression. He sweeps his eyes over his whole person, from head to foot, and then coolly resumes his former position and continues whispering to Martin. The look was a telling indictment, an expression of contempt and repugnance.*]

HAY:
General Wilkinson, how long and how well
Have you known the defendant, Colonel Burr?

WILKINSON:
Thirty years! Very well! Ever since Quebec.

HAY:
Did he confide to you his daring plan
To lead an expedition into Mexico?

151

WILKINSON:

    He told me he was raising troops to march
    Into Mexico, and then solicited
    My assistance in the undertaking.
    I told him I was only willing to join
    In case the President declared a war on Spain.

HAY:

    Tell the jury about the arsenal
    Where his troops were all preparing for that con-
      quest.

MARTIN:

    Your Honor, we object to that question.
    This is putting words into the witness' mouth.
    Let him tell all about the arsenal,
    If any such existed, which we deny!

THE CHIEF JUSTICE:

    Objection is sustained. Use your own words.

HAY:

    Tell in your own way all you know about
    Blennerhassett's Island, when were you there?

WILKINSON:

    I stopped at this island, March, Eighteen Five,
    At the urgent invitation of Colonel Burr.
    He told me it was to be his secret base
    For training troops to be sent to Mexico.

HAY:

    Did he train such troops, and later send them?

WILKINSON:

    He tried to, but I apprehended him
    Before the herds of the discontented
    And rebellious could join in seizing New Orleans.

HAY:

    When and where did you stop this invasion?

152

WILKINSON:
> On January twentieth, Eighteen Seven,
> At Bayou Pierre, in Mississippi.
> I sent three hundred trained militiamen
> To bring him to New Orleans for court martial,
> But he escaped on horseback, well-disguised.

HAY:
> What would have happened had you not interfered?

MARTIN:
> Your Honor, we object. This general is not
> God Almighty to know what would happen!

THE CHIEF JUSTICE:
> Objection is sustained. Just stick to facts.

HAY:
> Have you any further details to relate
> Of the prisoner's treason and treachery?

WILKINSON:
> I think by now the whole world knows the story.
> Colonel Burr, discredited in the East,
> Came West to organize a rebellion.
> He held out as bait two tricky incentives,
> One, the conquest of Mexico with himself
> As emperor; and the other hoax,
> The Washita Lands, which he claimed as his own,
> To be settled by his trained recruits —
> In case war on Spain was not declared.
> He tried in vain to inveigle my support,
> But I did not fall for his blandishments.

HAY:
> Your Honor, we are through with this witness.

MARTIN:
> Your Honor, may the defense cross-examine him?

*[The Chief Justice nods his head to proceed.]*

> Did you see with your own eyes any recruits

153

On that island, or can you testify
From your own knowledge that any existed there?

WILKINSON:

No, but everybody knows they existed.

MARTIN:

We have waited for you three long weeks
To come here, not to express your own opinion
But to state the facts from your own knowledge
As to the so-called organized rebellion
Of the West against the East, with Mexico
Thrown in – all engineered by Colonel Burr!
Now, General, will you kindly state the facts?

WILKINSON:

I've stated the facts and I can prove them true!

MARTIN:

That is exactly what the jury wants –
Proof that what you've said is based on facts.
Produce your proofs – for example, letters
From my client Colonel Burr, substantiating
Some or any one of your assertions.

WIRT:

Your Honor, we object to this request.

THE CHIEF JUSTICE:

I can see no reason for the objection.
If the witness can give some evidence
That his opinion of Colonel Burr's plans
Are correct, let him do so; otherwise
It is just one man's personal opinion.
We want facts that prove treason was committed.

MARTIN:

Did not Colonel Burr write you a letter
With reference to the expedition he planned
To transport troops to the city of Mexico?

WILKINSON:

It was long and very hard to decode!

It pointed out that the time had come to act,
Whether Jefferson declared war or not.
He asked me to join him in New Orleans
Last December, and march into Mexico.
He said that England would send ships and money,
That all classes along the Mississippi
Would join in the enterprise if I did.

AARON:
General, you say my letter was in code.
You have sworn to tell only the truth.
Did you alter it when you deciphered it?

WILKINSON [*Showing consternation*]:
Yes, parts of it which were too difficult.

AARON:
In other words, the copy of my letter
Which you sent the President was a forgery,
And marks you as a villain and a liar!
Your testimony is worthless in this case!

[*A great laugh goes through the crowd. The marshal
pounds with his gavel for silence. After a long inter-
val the jury and the audience are silent.*]

MARTIN:
Your honor, the defense is through with this witness,
Our very distinguished and trustworthy general,
Who has been in Spain's employ for many years.

[*Wilkinson is conducted from the room amid sup-
pressed boos from all sides and loud laughter.*]

HAY:
Your Honor, the prosecution is ready
To submit the case to this patient jury.

[*The Chief Justice nods his head in approval.*]

Gentlemen of the jury, we have clearly proved
An overt act of war by Aaron Burr,
On Blennerhassett Island, despite excuses.

The defendant organized a group of boys
To force a war on Spanish Mexico.
He counted on the discontents who live
Along the banks of the Mississippi River,
And also on the creoles of New Orleans,
To join his little band of mutineers.
His absurd excuse of the Washita Lands
Already has been shown to be a myth.
He has no claim to any such possession.
He was foiled in his crafty undertaking
By the astuteness of General Wilkinson,
Who had led him to divulge his base intent
To stir up a rebellion of the West
Against the East. Instead of standing trial,
The cowardly prisoner disguised himself and fled.
He intended to embark for England.
The President himself has frankly said
That "Of his guilt there cannot be a doubt."
What more evidence would any jury need?
I therefore ask this jury to declare
The prisoner to be guilty of high treason
Against the government, and to be hanged!

*[Hay mops his brow and takes his seat. There is a
tension of silence in the courtroom except for the
deep breathing and scattered sighs. Martin rises and
faces the jury.]*

MARTIN:
We too are ready to submit our case
To you patient gentlemen of the jury,
And we do so with the firmest confidence
That you will find our client innocent.
I do not suppose there ever was a case
Based on so much flimsy evidence,
Or such far-fetched, ridiculous reasoning.
To suggest that this defendant has committed
An act of treason is a base insult
To man's intelligence and sense of justice.
In fact it's a challenge to Almighty God

156

To strike down the defamers in His wrath.
I defy a single member of this jury
To cite just one particular brought out
In all the evidence submitted here
Which goes to prove the overt act of war.
Our client under oath denied the charge
That he had ever started any strife
Between the members of the United States,
And as for war with Mexico, he swore
That he, like General Jackson, was prepared
To strike, but only if the President
Decided to declare a war on Spain.

We know you will pronounce him not guilty.
He's actuated solely by desire
To serve his country and to make it great
Among the nations of this striving world.
He never has committed any crime.
This trial has been a solemn mockery,
An idle ceremony to transfer
A person's innocence from jail to gibbet
To gratify a popular desire
Stirred up by enemies who seek his death.

May God illuminate your understanding
And nerve your minds with fortitude and firmness,
That you may act according to His justice
And dispense it to your fellow citizen.

[*He bows to the Chief Justice and takes his seat. The Chief Justice turns to the jury.*]

THE CHIEF JUSTICE:
Gentlemen, you have heard the arguments
Of the counsel for both sides, also heard
The evidence they have submitted here.
You know this case is vitally important
Not alone because a life's at stake.
This case involves a principle of law
Far-reaching in our body politic.
For your guidance please remember only this,
All collateral evidence I now rule out.

157

To advise or procure a treasonable act
Is not considered treason in itself.
The overt act of treason on that island
Has either been established or has not.
You must decide by evidence submitted.
Your responsibility is to judge
And find a verdict, guilty or not guilty,
As your individual consciences direct.
You now will please withdraw and freely talk
Among yourselves. I hope you'll reach a verdict.

[*The jury is solemnly led out of the room by the marshal, while the Chief Justice keeps his seat, as do the attorneys and the audience. Loud whispers are heard on all sides. Aaron is talking to his attorneys by turns. All is tension and semi-silence. In a few minutes, the marshal enters the room and gives a message to the Chief Justice, who nods his head in approval. Thereupon the marshal leaves the room and almost immediately returns, directing the jurymen to their seats. Sudden and deep silence prevails.*]

THE CHIEF JUSTICE:
Gentlemen, have you now reached a verdict?

FOREMAN:
Your Honor, the jury has agreed — not guilty!

THE CHIEF JUSTICE:
I thank the jury for their close attention,
And your decision will now be recorded.
Goodbye to all. The court will stand adjourned.

[*The Chief Justice leaves the room.*]

[*A shout goes up and Colonel Burr's friends crowd around him, including several members of the jury, congratulating him. Aaron's face is beaming but careworn. After shaking hands with him, the crowds pass out and Aaron is left alone with his attorneys. He shakes hands cordially with each of them and thanks each for his wonderful support.*]

158

MARTIN:

Aaron, I predict that your indictment
For misdemeanor will be waived both here
And in Ohio, also in Kentucky,
Because they have no leg to stand upon —
And they know it — and so does Jefferson.

AARON:

I'll wait in Richmond for that verdict,
And then proceed to Philadelphia
To raise sufficient funds to go to England
And there, with Merry's help, solicit aid
To carry out my hoped for undertaking,
Of freeing Mexico from Spanish rule.

[*Then looking around in ecstasy at the faces of his
attorneys who have defended him through the long
trial, he shakes the hand of each again and expresses
his appreciation. All are enthusiastic and talking to
each other so that it is impossible to distinguish the
words being spoken.*]

AARON:

I ask you all to come to me tomorrow
At five o'clock and celebrate this day.
Meantime, I'll try to realize the difference
Between a verdict, guilty and not guilty!

[*Aaron turns to his desk to collect several sheets of
memoranda while his friends hastily depart. He is
startled by the rustling sound of a woman's dress.
Theo rushes down the aisle from the rear.*]

THEO:

I could hardly wait until they all had gone!
Oh, Father! Father! Now you're free at last!
This is the happiest day in all my life.

AARON:

Yes, now I'm free to reach my long-sought goal!
I know it will take time. I'll make the start!
Our boundaries must extend to the Pacific
And on the south take in all Mexico!

159

THEO:

Please, Father, take no risks! I'm so afraid!
Your powerful enemies still seek your life.

AARON:

As you know, I'll go to Europe soon,
And there I will secure a powerful backing.
My star will shine throughout all history!
Now let us leave this dreadful place at once.
The sight of these surroundings sickens me.

[*They hasten down the aisle toward the door.*]

CURTAIN

ACT FOUR

SCENE TWO

SCENE: *London, March 1, 1812. Library of the house
owned by the Honorable Jeremy Bentham, the great
philosopher of Utilitarianism. It is located on beautiful Saint James Park, London. A spacious room,
with crystal chandeliers, high ceilings with rococo
decorations, two walls lined with book shelves filled
with books, an Oriental carpet, mahogany writing
desk, ancestral portraits on the walls, heavy mahogany chairs, an open fireplace, over the mantel of
which hangs the portrait of Theodosia Burr Alston
in its narrow gilt frame.*

*Aaron and his friend, Jeremy Bentham, are seated on
opposite sides of the fireplace. Its burning logs light
up their faces. The hands of the tall clock register
five p. m. Two small tables, each with a decanter
of rum and several glasses, are placed by their
chairs. Both men are dressed in the height of fashion
— black silk small-clothes and neatly plaited hair,*

160

*white stocks, white ruffled shirts, white stockings and*
*black shoes with silver buckles.*

AARON:
The fact that I, at last, am to return
To my dear native land, America,
Is almost unbelievable; and yet
It saddens me to leave such friends as you.
I hope our paths will cross again and soon.
Your hospitality and constant deeds
Of kindness will not be forgotten soon.

BENTHAM:
It is to you that I owe gratitude.
I thank the Lord for bringing you to me.
Your wit has mollified my aging years.
As friend and brother, we view life alike;
We speak a common language, look on God
And stars and people with a common view.
I will miss you, Aaron, as a companion,
And so will all the many friends you've made.

AARON [*Looking at the portrait over the mantel*]:
You know it is my daughter's call to me!
Her love and true affection rule my life.
Her chief regret has been, she could not come
And share with me your hospitality.
She looks on you as second to no man,
Of ancient days or now. Your sound reasoning,
Your logic and your analytic thinking,
As author and philosopher, are such
That your books lie within her ready reach.
"Principles of Morals and Legislation"
Is her Bible. You must know her some day,
Jeremy! You will love her as I do.

BENTHAM:
Tut! Tut! Aaron, how you exaggerate!
Yet I confess I like your compliments.

161

AARON:

My indebtedness to you I cannot pay.
In your house I have met your brilliant friends,
Lady Holland, Lady Affleck and Charles Lamb,
And many more, including William Godwin.
My heart and mind will turn to you through life!

BENTHAM:

I have invited some of those dear friends
To come here for a farewell cup of tea
This afternoon — for they all are attached to you.

AARON:

That is delightful, friendship at its best!

BENTHAM:

Don't call it friendship. It is true affection!

AARON:

Say nothing more or I shall be in tears!
Your acts have strengthened my belief in God!
When I arrived in London four years ago,
I thought my world had really just begun.
I went to Canning, Castlereagh and Mulgrave,
The leaders of the British government.
I showed them how I'd conquer Mexico
And free it from the tyranny of Spain.
They all acknowledged my ability,
Apparently disposed to furnish funds.
I was summoned to appear for further talks.
Imagine my chagrin when I was told
To leave at once as undesirable!
I knew it was inspired by Jefferson.
My spirits sank! I knew not where to turn.
It was then that you first befriended me.
Your wise philosophy caused me to live!

BENTHAM:

I know you've had four most eventful years
In Belgium, Scotland, Holland, France and here.
I do not think your sojourn was in vain.

162

You now return with firsthand views of Europe
Which may enable you to gain your end.

AARON:

How wonderfully you read my inmost mind!
All depends upon my Theodosia.
Her confidence will give me strength to win.
I've stayed too long! My passports were denied!
But now that all is well I'll try again.
I've sounded depths, and scaled the heights in
  Europe!

BENTHAM:

At least, you scaled the heights in Edinburgh.

AARON:

Yes, there I knew McKenzie, Walter Scott
And members of their literary group.
I helped Sir Walter launch his famous book,
"The Lady of the Lake," through Ballantyne's,
The printing firm which I reorganized.
Those pleasant memories will last for life —
No matter what my fate may be at home.

BENTHAM:

Your situation baffles me, my friend.
Your friends respect and trust you over here,
And yet at home, you're hounded by a group
Who thwart your noble plans through ignorance.
How silly is our stupid human race!
Why can't they grasp my plan of utility?

AARON:

Because as yet we are not civilized.
The urge of sex and selfishness prevails.

BENTHAM:

I am surprised at your including sex
As one deterrent to man's craved ascent,
You who boast about your flair for women!

163

AARON [*Laughing*]:
　　And yet it is true, emotion dominates!
　　Sex is emotion! It has conquered reason.
　　To reach the God-like state which you portray,
　　We must subordinate our sex to reason.

BENTHAM:
　　Our scientists may someday solve the problem —
　　Science made practical! That is the trick!

AARON:
　　You know the God of Science is my God!

　　[*The butler enters and announces Mr. John Reeves.
　　Bentham and Aaron arise to greet him. They shake
　　hands and Bentham waves his two friends to chairs
　　and walks toward the door.*]

BENTHAM:
　　You two friends deserve an interview alone.
　　I shall return presently, so do sit down.

　　[*He leaves the room. Reeves takes a chair and Aaron
　　shows emotion and excitement.*]

AARON:
　　To think that this may be our final meeting
　　Fills me with sadness! In two days I sail.
　　I owe it to you that I have toured through Europe,
　　And now can go back home to start anew!
　　From my law practice I shall pay you all.

REEVES:
　　Sit down, Aaron, and calm yourself, my friend.
　　I know you want to pay me every dollar.
　　Please take your time. I am content to wait.
　　I invested in a cause and not in you —
　　A vision of a more enlightened world —
　　An end to all the tyranny of Spain —
　　Democracy in spirit, not merely words —
　　To end the hounding of a citizen,
　　A man of honor and high integrity,

164

By the witless prejudice of Jefferson!
What has happened to you since last we met?

[*Aaron offers Reeves a glass of brandy, fills one for
himself and they take chairs.*]

REEVES [*Continuing*]:
Now that is better, Aaron. Tell me all.

AARON:
Your financial backing has saved my life.
I owe my all to you and to my daughter.

REEVES:
What is her state of mind? Where is she now?

AARON:
Twice she has journeyed to New York to meet me.
As you know, my passport twice was lifted.
She is now back at home in South Carolina —
Her husband is the governor of that state.
Let me read you a passage from her letter.

[*Taking it out of his pocket, Aaron proceeds to read
it.*]

"Twelve months ago your letter came from Stock-
     holm.
Imagine my sad state of solitude —
Torn between my hope, my fear and grim despair!
My aching heart cries out, where is he now?
When shall we meet? That you are still engaged
In some most worthy cause is now my prayer —
The subject of my thoughts each day and night!"

REEVES:
It sounds more like a loving mother's letter.
It is, indeed, a rare relationship!
I hope that nothing will retard your meetings.
Now tell me all about your wanderings.

AARON:
My five months' stay in Gotenburg was heaven!

165

The galleries, the gardens, the stage —
The people all informal, friendly, kind!
My two American friends in banishment
Like me — Tom Robinson and Bill Hossack.

[*Lapsing into a reverie, with a faraway look in his eyes.*]

If you'll be patient, I shall tell you all!
Their youthful conversation, sparkling wit,
Their pretty wenches, filled my days and nights —
And then, whole days without a bite of food,
Until a chance remittance was received!
How I survived, I never can explain!
Then suddenly my passport was received,
Also one thousand marks from Swedish friends!
My life was saved! I hired a private rig —
No springs — its cushioned seats with strap supports —
A team of four black horses dashed me on!
A fortnight crowded with experiences!
I met Von Blucher of the war-machine —
The world will hear from him some fatal day —
Then Goethe, Wieland and Baroness de Stein.
They all became my friends and knew my child,
From Vanderlyn's fine portrait by my side.

Then came the news of Bonaparte's divorce.
A new alignment — France and Austria
Against Spain and England! This gave me new hope.
With vivid dreams I hastened straight to Paris.
If I could meet Napoleon, I would win!
He would adopt my plan for Mexico!
With five hundred volunteers I'd easily snatch
The Bahamas from Old England in a month,
Then take New Orleans and all Mexico!
But Bonaparte was unapproachable.
For months he kept me in uncertainty,
I wrote my secret plan in duplicate,
Prepared to leave a copy in his hands.
Talleyrand, my friend, could see to this —
Or Jerome Bonaparte — they both had often dined

166

At my house in New York. They owed me much!
Alas, they both were cowed by Jefferson!

At the Theatre Francais, I tried a ruse.
The Emperor was standing in his box,
As usual bowing to the long applause.
The play had ended. This was now my chance!
Through bribery and stealth I reached the street.
(The audience kept back for half an hour.)
I forced myself in line with all the guards
And next to Duke Rovigo, chief of police.
In my excitement I revealed my plan!
His contact with the Emperor was such
That he assured me he would place my note
Within his hands. In faith I gave it up!
That was the end! I wasted six more weeks.
The Duke then sent a most insulting note:
"A fugitive from justice had no claim
Except surrender to the courts for trial!"

Another passport gained and I embarked!
The British seized my ship, the *Vigilante*.
I forfeited my money for the voyage,
And have been kept in England ever since.
But now, at last, I have another chance!

[*Aaron heaves a deep sigh and comes out of his reverie; he springs to his feet and paces up and down
the room.*]

REEVES [*Having watched with anxiety this strange be-
havior*]:
There never was so strange a case as yours —
A dignified heredity, lucid brain,
Companion of the founders of the States,
Statesman, Senator, then Vice President,
Tried for treason and found innocent,
Associate of all the world's great men,
But having at the same time strange amours
With lowly barmaids and with princesses!
Looked upon by some as patriotic,
By others as a scoundrel and a thief!

167

It is the paradox of history!
I know your heart is true and hope that fate
Will yet enable you to bring about
Your noble plans for the United States.

AARON:
That you have faith in me despite my faults
Inspires me to pursue my uphill fight.
My chief incentive to restore my place
In the estimation of this silly world
Is to prove to my daughter that her faith
Is not in vain. May I read three more lines?

REEVES:
Most certainly. I'd love to hear some more.

AARON [*Taking the letter from his pocket and reading*]:
"I witness your brave attitude with wonder!
At every new misfortune you seem to me
So superior, so elevated
Above all other men on this our earth!
I think of you with strange humility,
With admiration, reverence and pride,
And it would take but little superstition
To make me worship you as I do Christ,
Such enthusiasm you arouse in me!"

[*Wiping his eyes.*]

Is it any wonder I carry on?

REEVES [*Looking at the clock and jumping from his chair*]:
Now I must go; but let us keep in touch.
I stole away to wish you bon voyage.
Forget about the money. Be at ease!

AARON:
You'll hear from me the day that I reach home,
And later when my ship of state comes in.

[*At this moment Bentham returns surrounded by a number of guests, all of whom speak to Reeves as he*

168

*passes out through the door, then rush up to Aaron, shake his hand, pat his shoulder and show close friendship. All are talking at once. And then the confusion dies down].*

LADY AFFLECK [*Looking at Aaron*]:
We're going to miss you very much, my friend —
Your naughty sallies and your specious lies —

[*Looking at the portrait.*]

But we know your heart is always with your daughter.

AARON:
I can only tell your ladyship
My dearest wish is that she may meet you.

GODWIN [*Looking at Aaron*]:
Now you are flattering her ladyship,
As though you were a blatant Irishman.
Will any luckless female on your ship
Escape from all your subtle blandishments?

[*Everybody laughs at this and Aaron, happy to be the center of attention, turns to Charles Lamb, the popular young author who has been trying to speak.*]

LAMB:
I can see him writing seducing notes
To all the pretty women on the ship.

AARON:
Far from it! I shall likely be engaged
In reading your enchanting "Tales from Shakespeare,"
A copy of which is now packed in my trunk;
Or trying to decipher at long last
Godwin's "Enquiry Concerning Justice —"
Whether political or otherwise.
If I could once contrive to understand
And come to his conclusions, I might then
Find a way to forgive Thomas Jefferson!

169

*[This sally brings long and loud laughter from all present.]*

BENTHAM:
My friends, before this farewell party grows
Into a clash of arms, let us sit down
And try some of my favorite special brandy
Before it all evaporates in air.

*[They all take seats and the butler passes a tray of glasses and decanters. They help themselves and there is a hum of conversation while the glasses are being filled.]*

LAMB:
I often wonder what would have occurred
If Aaron had had his talk with Napoleon.

GODWIN:
Or better still, with lovely Josephine
Before she lost her influence at court.

BENTHAM:
I daresay Napoleon would then have said,
"Go quick and conquer Mexico for France!"

MARY LAMB *[Sister of Charles and dressed in the height of fashion]*:
Charles, you are to blame for all of this
Foolish talk when Aaron is leaving us.

AARON:
My dearest lady, if you only knew
How much I welcome this delightful chatter,
Instead of sad farewells and falling tears!
Besides, who knows what might have come to pass
Had Napoleon granted me an audience?
I had much to offer had he only known it!

*[They all laugh heartily. While this conversation has been going on, Godwin's daughter, Mary, aged 16, and Percy Bysshe Shelley, aged 20, have been*

170

*standing apart in whispered conversation. Godwin,*
*glancing at them, shows his impatience.*]

GODWIN:
Mary, my dear, you've forgotten your host.
How long will you desert our company?

MARY [*Impulsively*]:
Father, I apologize. It's all my fault!
Percy has just told me some shocking news.
I wanted to hear it all while it is fresh.
Although he ranks the first within his class,
And never has been even criticized,
He was yesterday expelled from Oxford
Because he circulated his pamphlet
Entitled, "The Necessity of Atheism."

[*A loud murmur of astonishment escapes from all
present.*]

BENTHAM:
Percy, tell us what has happened to you!

SHELLEY:
Mary has told you all there is to tell.
We've gone back to the days of intolerance
At Oxford! An individual no longer
Possesses any freedom of expression —
Unless it suits the faculty's good pleasure!
I am red hot, and I will make a fight!
They will suffer for their narrow attitude!

BENTHAM:
What are you planning to do about all this?

SHELLEY:
I'll expose their narrow-mindedness
Upon the lecture platform everywhere.
David O'Connell has invited me
To address the popular Assembly any time.
I told him I would go to Dublin next week.
They'll all be sorry they have started this!

171

AARON:
  Percy, don't be discouraged; you are right!
  But remember you are launching an attack
  And that you're not promoting "intolerance."
  To me it seems a matter of definition!

  [*Looking around the group.*]

  I think each one of us has his own God.
  Percy's definition is "Atheism" —
  So let it go at that! And mine is "Science!"
  We have a right to our sincere opinions.

LADY AFFLECK:
  Though Aaron speaks the truth, we should unite
  In forcing Oxford to be tolerant.
  To think that our great university
  Should teach intolerance arouses fear!

GODWIN:
  Percy, I shall gladly join in your crusade.
  We know that something governs the universe.
  We call it "God," but it's incredulous
  To think God is a person like ourselves.
  No one can ever know just what it is.
  If we could find that out, we'd all be Gods.

MRS. ACHAUD [*Rising and looking at the clock*]:
  My friends, this is all very interesting,
  Unfortunately I, for one, must take my leave.

  [*They all rise.*]

LAMB:
  Aaron, why don't you come along with me?
  There is so much I want to say to you.

AARON:
  Thanks, my friend, but I must stay with Jeremy.
  God only knows when I will see him again —
  Or any of you — but you will all remain
  A vital part of life in days to come!

172

[*He says this with much emotion.*]

DAME BARTLETT:

    Brace up, Aaron! We hate to have you go,
    But want to remember you with smiles — not tears!

AARON:

    Perhaps that's for the best! I dread farewells!
    I thank you all for coming, and your friendship
    Makes life worth living. We will meet again.

[*They all crowd around Aaron, in their friendly way,
and the hum of their voices drowns out their words.
After they all depart, Aaron returns to the room,
stands by the fire, then pours himself a glass of
brandy, sits down and soliloquizes.*]

AARON:

    So this is Aaron Burr now gone to seed!
    These English friends enabled me to live.
    I contemplated suicide in France
    When, after months of waiting, I perceived
    That Napoleon's ministers were doubled-faced,
    Pretending that an audience was near.
    Napoleon did not dare to risk my plan.
    His hands were tied by England and Spain.
    That was the end of all my cherished dreams.
    The Spanish colonies will yet be free —
    When I am dead and gone! I missed my chance!
    An exile from my native land, a beast
    Exposed to every trap the law could spring!
    No wonder that I sank in self-esteem —
    An opium fiend, a worthless parasite!
    For months I starved and daily prayed for death —
    And then that letter from my darling child!
    I braced myself for her. So here I am
    About to start another phase of life!
    With Jefferson retired and Madison
    Asleep, I may recoup my wasted years.
    I'll give up politics and stick to law!
    The hundred thousand dollars that I owe

Will all be paid. From beggar I shall turn
A millionaire and prove to all my worth!
A lawyer's at his prime at fifty-six!
With Theodosia and her son alive,
I may have twenty years of usefulness.
I dare not go to them direct. New York
Will harbor me and there we shall unite!
I'll summon them when I have docked at Boston.
Perhaps they both can meet me at the dock.
Pray God that all goes well with both of them!
They must not know that I was profligate.
I'll find a way to make them proud of me!

## CURTAIN

# ACT FOUR

## SCENE THREE

SCENE: *New York law office, November, 1819. Six
years later. The law office of Aaron Burr on Reade
Street, New York. It is about eighteen feet square, a
fireplace with logs burning, Theo's portrait over the
wooden mantel, a door and two windows, high ceiling, book shelves, an ancient baise table in the center
of the room. It is a cozy, comfortable looking room.
Aaron, now 62, has aged greatly in appearance. His
hair is almost white. He has grown stout. His face is
creased with lines, and his features have become
blurred, with heavy jowls and puffs under the eyes.
He has the look of a man without ambition. His eyes
are embittered and they show his inner resentment
behind a pose of cynical indifference. His black-
rimmed glasses are propped above his forehead in his
hair.*

174

*His two old friends, Colonel Robert Troup and Samuel Swartwout, about his age, but both much taller, are seated around the table. All are dressed in small-clothes, with white stocks, white stockings and low black shoes. Both his friends have kind eyes and a benevolent cast of features. They look at Aaron with compassion; sincere friendliness is shown in their expressions and manner. On one side of the desk are three letter boxes, each with locks. One of them is open. Aaron holds a letter in one hand, in the other is a huge cigar which he keeps puffing intermittently.*

SWARTWOUT [*Looking at Aaron*]:
That last letter you read was fascinating —
So full of wit. Do read some more of them.
You're very fortunate to have these records
Portraying history. They keep you young —
Also your friends, who gather in your office.

AARON:
Sam, I thank God and you for this office.
And you, Bob, for these law books.
What would I have done without such friends!

TROUP:
I had just retired when you returned
And was glad to turn those books over to you.

AARON [*Holding out the letter in his hand to Swartwout*]:

This is a recent one from Venezuela
Authorizing me to raise land and sea troops
To help in throwing off the shackles of Spain.
Please read the lines which I have underscored.

SWARTWOUT [*Takes the paper, puts on his glasses, clears his throat and reads*]:

"Governor's Palace, Angostura, October 9, 1819.
"To whom it may concern: I, John Baptiste, Cap-

175

tain General of the Armies and Vice President, in
compliance with the duty imposed upon me in the
absence of the President, do hereby authorize Aaron
Burr, a citizen of the United States, to raise troops
for sea and land services to aid this Government now
struggling in the cause against the despotism of
Spain; and that the said Aaron Burr may legally exert
himself in favor of the emancipation and liberty of
Venezuela, and New Granada, and all other countries
in South America and Mexico.
"Signed with my hand and sealed with the seal of
the Republic of Venezuela."

TROUP:

Splendid! You showed me a Mexican letter
From General Toledo, offering you
The leadership of the revolutionists
Of that country — I think in Eighteen Sixteen.
Both were certainly great compliments.

AARON:

Yes, that's the date. Had Theo been alive
I should have seized those opportunities
Of carrying out my plans. They came too late!
I realized my life in politics had ended,
And regretfully declined them both.

SWARTWOUT:

When all is said and done the law is better.
The Lord was with you! I shall never forget
How your clients flocked around you overnight
When Aaron Burr once more hung out his shingle!

AARON:

It was all wonderful but not a miracle!
A half dozen friends, including you,
Not only saved my life by sending clients
But enabled me to pay all pressing debts.
Yes, I owe it all to my devoted friends!

[*They are interrupted by a knock at the door. Colo-*

176

*nel Troup goes to the door and is joined by Swart-
wout.*]

AARON [*Left alone, exclaims aloud*]:
  I see that pirate ship extend its hooks
  And quickly board the little *Patriot.*
  Fierce, bearded bandits grab my little girl
  And drag her by the hair, perhaps — who knows —
  Then satisfy their wild, barbaric lusts!
  I hear her screams, half smothered in those beards.
  I see her struggle in those savage arms.
  I see her ship now scuttled, slowly sink,
  While she is carried to the Barbary Coast!
  And I am daily crucified by thoughts!
  Why is it God decrees that I should live?

[*Meantime, his friends having opened the door and
admitted Luther Martin, very much under the influence of liquor, his eyes bleary and his heavy face
blotched and repulsive, stand speechless, listening to
Aaron's monologue in amazement.*]

TROUP [*Stepping forward*]:
  Aaron, what's the matter? Have you lost your mind?

AARON [*Returning to his chair and taking up his cigar
from the tray*]:
  Forgive me! I'm sorry! It's about Theo!
  Whenever I think of her I lose my mind!
  Have terrible visions! Perhaps I'm insane!

[*Turning to Martin.*]
  Martin, have a chair. Is anything wrong?

MARTIN [*Remaining standing without removing his
hat, while the others take chairs*]:
  I thought you were alone. I've lost my purse,
  And came to ask you to lend me ten dollars.

AARON [*Taking ten dollars from his purse and handing
it to Martin*]:
  Certainly. I'm glad to let you have it.

177

MARTIN:
Thanks a lot. I shall return it soon —
When I find my purse. Goodbye, gentlemen.

[*He staggers to the door and goes out.*]

TROUP:
A sad case! A worthless drunken sot!
And once he headed the bar of America!

SWARTWOUT [*With indignation*]:
Aaron, I think you're going too far in this case!
You give him room and board and money for whis-
key.

AARON:
But for him, I might have been hung for treason.
There's nothing too much that I can do for him.
The doctors say he can't survive much longer!

TROUP:
We know he'd be locked up except for you!

SWARTWOUT [*Looking squarely in Aaron's face*]:
Your friends all think you spend too lavishly.

AARON:
I only give my money to the needy!
I know just what it means to starve and beg!
I still owe thousands to friends who rescued me —
My wealthy friends including Reeves and Bentham.
I'll pay them all when I have made a strike.
Meantime I've paid my enemies in full.

TROUP:
There is a limit to generosity.
Is it true you've given within the last four weeks
A thousand dollars to your indigent friends?

AARON:
Now see here, Bob, where did you hear that tale?

[*His friends laugh heartily.*]

178

TROUP:
    We laugh because you are so clever at law,
    But when it comes to money, you're a child!
    It's time for you to face your greatest fault —
    Unless you choose a penniless old age!

AARON:
    Well, I must be only what I am!
    When I earn money, I do as I like!

TROUP:
    Of course you have that right! You've been superb!
    You've conquered life! So why not now conserve it?

AARON:
    I have not conquered life! My mind's distrait!
    I was a coward when I first returned.
    I should have gone to Theo instantly —
    Especially when she wrote her son had died!
    What difference would it make had I been seized?
    Better far than what has happened since!

SWARTWOUT:
    Your friends all know you did what you thought best.

AARON:
    I sent to her my trusted friend, Tim Greene,
    To bring her to New York by merchant ship.
    She was too shocked and ill to come by land.
    It all took time, but finally they sailed
    December thirty-first, Eighteen Twelve,
    On the little merchant schooner, *Patriot*.
    To think that that was seven years ago!
    As you well know, the ship was lost at sea!

SWARTWOUT: [*Knowing Aaron's preoccupation with his
    letter boxes*]:
    Now read us more from your prized letter boxes.

TROUP:
    Yes, we came to share some of your secrets.

                                                    179

AARON [*Taking several letters from the open box*]:
  You know I love to share them with such friends.
  Here is a fatal one from Timothy Greene
  Dated at Georgetown, December,
      Eighteen Twelve.

  [*He reads in a trembling voice*]:

  "Our passage to New York has been engaged
  For your daughter in a sturdy pilot boat,
  Which has been privateering in these waters
  But is now refitted and seaworthy.
  Mrs. Alston is fully bent on going.
  Don't be surprised by her feeble appearance.
  Her complaint is incessant nervous fever.
  Will take at least five or six days more.
  Captain Overstocks commands the *Patriot*
  And Mister Cook is an old New York pilot."

  [*His friends show concern for Aaron's nervous condition but remain silent as he takes up another letter.*]

  This one happens to be from my son-in-law,
  Joseph Alston, dated at Charleston,
  February twenty-fifth, Eighteen Thirteen.
  "When I turned from the grave of my poor boy,
  I deemed myself no longer vulnerable.
  How wrong! For now I suffer torments of Hell!
  My wife was either captured or was lost!
  You say you're severed from the human race!
  But I'm the spirit of desolation —
  My only wish, that I might join the dead!"

SWARTWOUT: [*Interrupting*]:
  Please read a few political letters.

TROUP:
  And a few from some of your lady loves!

AARON:
  I only picked these up at random;
  I certainly don't want to bore either of you.

180

SWARTWOUT:

You are not boring us in the least.
What's in the other one you took from the box?

AARON:

It's one I wrote Governor Alston, Eighteen Fifteen:
"A Congressional caucus plans to nominate
James Monroe for President next month.
This seems to me exceptionally odious,
And hostile to an independent suffrage.
A junto of fictitious Virginians
Considers the United States their property.
Their principle art, which was taught by Jefferson,
Is that of causing a state of dissension!
Monroe is stupid, illiterate, hypocritical!
His character exactly suits this junto!"

[*His friends burst into loud laughter.*]

TROUP:

Aaron, you're unpredictable! Do read the rest.

AARON:

Well, since you are not bored, I shall continue.
"It now is time for you, dear Governor Alston,
To act. Assert yourself and make them fear you!
Thus far they seem to think that you fear them.
We know that offices are now bestowed
For power alone, without regard to fitness.
The time is ripe to break down this vile system.

I know one man of firmness and decision.
It is your solemn duty to proclaim him.
That man is Andrew Jackson, strong and virile.
His nomination should be made at once
Before the Virginia faction has its say.
A resolution by your Legislature
Will save our country from this base attempt.
You owe it to yourself and to the dead
To take prompt action in this worthy cause."

[*He lays the letter aside and looks earnestly at his
friends for their comments.*]

181

TROUP:
Aaron, I think that letter is magnificent!
We now know Jackson was the better man,
And I predict that some day he'll be President!

SWARTWOUT:
Do you have at hand the Governor's reply?

AARON [*Looking through his papers*]:
Yes, here is his reply — a whole year later:
"Your letter came too late for me to act;
But even had it come in time, dear sir,
It would have found me utterly collapsed,
Incapable of earnest execution!
I fully coincide with your remarks,
But spirit, health and energy were lacking!
I was and still continue unconnected
With world affairs. I now belong to death!"

TROUP:
How disappointing! The death of his poor wife,
Following his son's, had ruined his career!

AARON [*Sighing deeply*]:
Yes, he died soon after writing this letter.

[*A knock is heard at the door and Colonel Troup
rises to admit a young boy of six, a middle-aged
woman, well-dressed, and two very pretty and stylish-
ly gowned young girls of about eighteen and twenty.
They enter the room with vivacity and all rush up
and kiss Aaron, who lays his cigar aside and cordially
greets them.*]

This is Colonel Troup and Mister Swartwout.

[*Then turning to his two friends.*]

This is my very dear friend, Mrs. Eden,
For whom I won an important law case,
And her daughters, Rebecca and Elizabeth,
Whose education I am now directing.

And this is Charles Burdett, my adopted son.
This little group has filled the gap in my life
Left by the death of Theodosia.

[*Meantime, Colonel Troup and Mr. Swartwout are shaking hands with the newcomers, all smiling pleasantly.*]

MRS. EDEN:

We thought you were expecting us at home.
Your maid told us to come to your office.
I fear we are interrupting a conference.

AARON:

You are most welcome. Here are the papers.

[*Handing one to Rebecca and one to Elizabeth.*]

They're nearly perfect. You're both making progress.
Only two misspelled words! I'm proud of you both!
I have outlined plans for your next essays,
And I'll see you next week here or at home.
We shall then go over them personally.

MRS. EDEN:

Colonel Burr, words can't express my gratitude
For what you're doing for my daughters.
You're making self-reliant women of them.

AARON:

Tut, tut! It is I who am indebted to them
For enabling me to indulge my hobby!
I love to teach, also to prove to the world
That woman's intellect is equal to man's!

MRS. EDEN [*Rising*]:

We must go! We must not interrupt you!
We're glad to meet your friends. Hope they excuse
  us!

[*As they move toward the door, Aaron shakes hands with each, then puts his arm around Charles and gives him a hug.*]

183

CHARLES [*Looking lovingly at Aaron*]:
When will you be home, Father? I'll wait for you.

AARON:
Not till five o'clock! I'll bring you a puzzle.

[*They leave and Aaron closes the door.*]

TROUP:
It's fine you have this outlet! They're all charming!
I'm glad to have this insight into your life.

SWARTWOUT [*Taking their two hats from the rack*]:
We must be going but will return next week,
And hope you'll read us more from your treasure
trove.

AARON:
Thanks for coming! I'll expect you both next week.
I'm trying to forget that great mystery!
I can't control myself when Theo's mentioned!
I fear the obsession will endure for life.

TROUP:
We understand perfectly! It could be worse!
We three are alive! I hope we'll last for years!

AARON [*Looking at his watch as they go out*]:
I have a client due in twenty minutes.
I'm ready for him! See you next week! Goodbye!

[*He places his letters in the box and locks it, then begins to pace the floor.*]

They think that I'm insane! Perhaps I am!
That dreadful scene still haunts me day and night!
I see her standing on the deck in terror,
Clinging to the rail, as waves engulf the ship!
Her cries to man and prayers to God unheard!
She sees dead bodies floating round the ship,
Or floating out to feed the hungry sharks!
At last the vessel rolls upon its side!

184

My Theo swallowed by the foaming sea!
I hear her cry, "Dear Father, join me soon!"

CURTAIN

# ACT FOUR

## SCENE FOUR

SCENE: *Winant's Inn. Seventeen barren years have elapsed. It is midafternoon of Wednesday, September 14, 1836. The whole stage is occupied by the bedroom of Aaron Burr at Winant's Inn, in the village of Port Richmond, Staten Island, New York. He has chosen this abode because his cousin, Judge Ogden Edwards, lives near, and also because he can have the Winant family attention. The portrait of his daughter hangs over the fireplace. It is lighted by the sun rays which are pouring through the window. Two candles are beneath it on the wooden mantel, not yet lighted. His bed is arranged so that he faces the portrait.*

*It is a large, comfortable room and, through the window, the outlines of the tall buildings of New York City can be seen in the distance. In one corner, next to his bed, a flat-top desk is piled high with letter boxes. An armchair is on one side of the fireplace, where huge logs are burning brightly. Several chairs are placed around the room and a clothes cupboard occupies one side of the wall. A large, homespun brown rug covers the floor. A chandelier hangs from the ceiling, and the sun rays are reflected from its prisms.*

185

*Aaron is propped up in bed and looks emaciated. The bony structure of his head and cheeks and jaws and his pallid color combine to make him look like a ghost. His brilliant eyes are as sparkling as ever and have become even more keen. The room is filled with visitors — John Vanderlyn, the artist who painted Theo's portrait, is sitting by the bed; Robert Troup, Judge Edwards, Samuel Swartwout are standing at the foot of the bed engaged in conversation.*

*Aaron Columbus Burr and Charles Burdett are seated on the opposite side of the room, near the window, in deep conversation. They are about twenty-two years of age and both very handsome, with Aaron's features. Charles is dressed in the uniform of the Navy.*

CHARLES:
Our father has supreme vitality.
The doctor said he'd not survive the night,
Yet here he is — and much improved today!

COLUMBUS:
How do you know he is your father?
I thought you were an adopted son!

CHARLES:
He told me yesterday I was his son.

COLUMBUS:
It seems that since he knows his end is near,
He's telling all of us our true relation!

CHARLES:
We are all proud of father. I know I am!
Have you seen our two half-sisters, eight years old?

COLUMBUS:
No! Have you? I hear they're very pretty.

CHARLES:
Yes, they both are beauties. Look like father!

186

COLUMBUS:
How many of us are there? Do you know?

CHARLES:
I estimate there are twenty or twenty-five.

[*They both laugh so that the others in the room turn
and look at them.*]

COLUMBUS:
We'd better go and leave him with his friends.
I'm afraid we are disturbing them.
So many came when they heard he was dying!
The strain on him must be considerable!

[*They leave the room quietly after looking keenly
at Aaron, who does not seem to notice them.*]

AARON [*Addressing Vanderyln*]:
They are my adopted sons. They came to see me
When they heard I was dying. I'll fool them all!

VANDERLYN:
How many adopted children have you, Aaron?

AARON:
I really do not know. It gives me pleasure
To help them with their education,
And to get them started in the world.

[*Turning his eyes to the portrait of his daughter.*]

You have given me my greatest pleasure —
This lovely portrait of my daughter!
It has never left my side in forty years!

VANDERLYN:
I'm very happy to have painted it!

AARON:
If you survive me, kindly have it hung
At Princeton! As you know, that's in my will!

187

VANDERLYN:
   You may outlive us all! No one can tell!
   Now I must go; but I'll return quite soon.

   [*He pats Aaron's shoulder and starts toward the door.*]

JUDGE EDWARDS:
   Wait a minute! I'll accompany you.

   [*Then turning to Aaron.*]

   You look much better now than yesterday.
   Don't worry! I'll attend to your bequests —
   That is, if I outlive you! Just relax!
   Don't see too many friends! An enigma
   Is what your Doctor Hossack calls your case.

AARON [*Laughing*]:
   I know that he thought I would die last June!

EDWARDS:
   You may recover just as you did then!
   Send for me anytime you want me. Goodbye!

AARON:
   Thank you, Ogden. You have all been good to me.
   See to it that I'm buried at Princeton
   Beside my father and my grandfather!

   [*He feebly waves his hand as Vanderlyn and Judge Edwards leave the room, then turns to Troup and Swartwout.*]

   Now we are alone. Bring up your chairs
   And let us have one of our old time talks.
   Life would not be worth living without you!

TROUP:
   You have a host of friends — remember that!

AARON:
   Ridiculous! You know that is not true!
   When I returned from Europe years ago,

188

The Federalists shunned me — I had shot their idol!
About a dozen of my thousand friends
Welcomed me! The others turned their backs —
I was a public curiosity —
The man whom Thomas Jefferson called a traitor
And tried for treason! I'm an outcast!

SWARTWOUT:

Forget all that, since you were proven innocent!

AARON:

I know and you know that I should just as soon
Have thought of taking the moon and dividing it
Among my friends as foolishly attempting
A division of these United States!

TROUP:

Aaron, we know you have been terribly maligned,
But you have many friends still true to you —
And many of them are even in Texas!

AARON:

The world knows I was right about Texas!
What was treason then is patriotism now!

SWARTWOUT:

You were thirty years ahead of your time!
Your trouble all was due to Jefferson!

AARON:

I've always failed in every undertaking,
But in the end, results have proved me right!
You know, because, Bob, you were on the ground,
That Canada would now belong to us
Had Montgomery just followed out my plan!

TROUP:

Yes, I really think that that is true!

AARON:

And Mexico would now belong to us
If Jefferson had taken my advice
Instead of being fooled by Wilkinson.

189

SWARTWOUT:

    That is debatable — I mean the word "now";
    It would eventually have been a part
    Of the United States. Of that I'm sure!

[*They all three laugh heartily.*]

AARON:

    As for Texas, Florida and California,
    I know as well as I'm living
    They would have been new states or territories
    Long before this time — and much blood spared —
    Had I been President instead of Jefferson —
    At least allowed to execute my plan!

TROUP:

    Historians will discover this someday,
    And then your name will shine throughout the ages!
    You will become a persecuted martyr!

AARON:

    I only hope you're right! I'll not be here
    To have that satisfaction! Columbus died
    Not knowing that his name would live forever!

[*He becomes excited, his eyes flashing, then looks at the setting sun.*]

    Of what difference is it in the long run,
    Who we are or what we are in life's brief span?
    A sense of satisfaction with our work,
    The knowledge that our hearts are always right —
    That makes this life worth living, and dying sweet!
    My mad frivolities I do not count
    As weighing in the devil's scales against me!
    My life was consecrated to a cause —
    Desire to see my country rank supreme,
    And to worship at the shrines of my dear ones!
    So let it go at that! I'll take my chances
    In the world to come, because I know God's just!
    I am not conscious that I ever harmed
    A human being during my whole life!

190

TROUP:
Do you mean that that includes Hamilton?

AARON:
To shoot a man, I feel is not a crime
If done according to accepted codes!
The earth provided space for both of us,
And he, not I, brought on that foolish duel!
He died, and I have suffered hell's torments!
Which one is better off? At least it cured the world
Of that ridiculous childishness called duels!
The world is now my bitter enemy,
But, strange as it may seem, I'm still its friend!

[*He tries to sit up straight, but falls back in the pillows. A maid comes into the room.*]

Bring in some grog and glasses for my friends,
And, if you please, bring me a big cigar!

TROUP [*To the maid aside*]:
Pay no attention! His mind is soaring!

MAID:
Will you have some grog, sir? I can get it!

TROUP:
No, thank you very much! Leave him to us.

[*The maid goes out.*]

SWARTWOUT:
You've won some famous lawsuits, earned large fees,
And helped your friends in trouble, these twenty
    years!

AARON:
That's good of you, my friend, but I have failed!
I was swamped by clients twenty years ago,
But now I only live upon my pensions
And half-pay as a colonel in the Army!

SWARTWOUT:
You have reason to be proud of your life.

191

AARON:

I have no legal child to bear my name!
My wife, my daughter and my little grandson
Are out there in the sunshine to welcome me!
That stroke six years ago should have released me!

TROUP:

I never heard you morbid in my life!
Let us enjoy life while we are here!

AARON:

My marriage to Eliza Jumel finished me!
I longed for tenderness and consolation,
Companionship and sympathy and love —
Someone who shared my zeal for education!
And then Eliza came and sprang her trap!

TROUP:

Why, with your experience, did you marry her?

AARON:

I thought she offered me security!
She inherited that handsome mansion
Left her by her husband, the wine merchant,
Also an income which she asked me to share.
She knew I'd just recovered from a stroke.
That made no difference! She wanted my name!
What could I do but seize the opportunity,
Despite my mental reservations!
So we were married July, Eighteen Thirty-three!

SWARTWOUT:

What ever came between you to cause divorce?

AARON:

She asked me to invest her income!
I put six thousand dollars in the stock
Of that new bridge company which shortly failed.
Despite my explanation, she was angry.
And then the second week, unfortunately,
I lost ten thousand dollars by pure accident
And was forced to sell her handsome new hackneys

For five hundred dollars to raise the cash
To pay the servants' wages for the week.
She claims the hackneys cost a thousand dollars!
We had such bitter words I left her house!
I think that this brought on my second stroke.
She came and took me back and I recovered.

TROUP:
It is indeed a most romantic tale!
Did you lose any more of her money?

AARON:
She never let me handle another cent!
It was not the money, though, which caused divorce!

TROUP:
What was it then? You make me curious!

AARON:
She has a gorgeous creature for a maid. —
And, following my habit of a lifetime,
One day I tried to feel her lovely leg.
The silly girl went screaming from the room
And told Eliza that she'd have to leave!
What could I do? I tried to laugh it off!
Eliza knows my foibles perfectly!
She slammed the door and locked it in my face.
Next day she entered suit for our divorce.

SWARTWOUT [*Looking very glum*]:
Has it been granted? Will you make a fight?

AARON:
The decree had not been rendered when I left.
I found this inn and moved to it at once.
Eliza may come after me someday
When she has realized her foolish act!

TROUP:
I am amazed! It's not like normal life!

AARON:
My life has never been quite normal, Bob!

193

From birth I've suffered many handicaps!
No mother to protect me as a child!
Another handicap has been my pride!

TROUP:

I know, of course, we're victims of our fate.
With each of us heredity plays its part!
It made of you almost a superman —
The dream of all philosophers and saints!

AARON:

A dream, you say! Yes, that is the word for it.
Having failed to annex Canada,
I dreamed that I could bring in the Southwest.
I pray to God my dream may yet come true!

TROUP:

You can do nothing more! So rest in peace
And realize that someday this old world
May put you on the pedestal of history
And statesmanship where I think you belong!

AARON:

All this is dulcet music to my ears,
But truth prevails! My failure to accomplish
My objectives has put me in my place!
It is the law of life! I'm not practical!
I possess the mental ability —
Even willingness to sacrifice my life —
But failed to judge Washington and Jefferson —
My inferiors — and yet they won!
Enough of this! You came to charm me back
To health by your devoted friendship —
So let us talk of pleasant things — not my woes!

[*A loud knock is heard and all are startled. The maid
enters the room greatly agitated and looks at Aaron.*]

MAID:

A lady wants to see you, sir, at once.

[*Eliza Burr enters in a fury. She looks like a witch
although she is dressed in the extreme fashion of the
day, and her diamond broach and earrings and the*

194

*rings on her waving hands flash brilliantly. The maid hastily departs.*]

ELIZA:

Am I intruding? If so I shall wait!

SWARTWOUT [*Rising with Troup and looking at Aaron in consternation*]:

Certainly not, madam. We are just leaving.
We've been paying a visit to your husband.

ELIZA:

Aaron, here is the decree! We are divorced!
No longer can you claim I owe you board!
I heard that you were dying, but it seems
You're indulging in an old-time drinking bout!
Why I ever married you, I do not know.
Never darken the threshold of my house again!
Here is the decree, all signed and sealed!
You are now free to go to hell and find
Companionship with all your paramours!

[*She throws the paper on the bed and dashes out of the room, and Aaron sinks back in the pillows looking stunned.*]

AARON:

Well, at least I am departing this sad life
In peace and in the arms of my well-wishers.

[*His friends look at him and at each other in amazement.*]

SWARTWOUT:

Her conduct is unheard-of! It's outrageous!
Where did she come from and where did she go?
What devil spirit is abroad tonight?

AARON [*Clutching the divorce papers in his hand*]:
Now go, my friends. Take not my sufferings
Too much to heart. This final state is not
The end of my misfortunes and my life.

195

[*He turns his eyes to the setting sun which is now going down into the sea in a great blazing light. Then he closes his eyes and sinks limp, with his right hand over his heart. Apparently he has fainted. Colonel Troup loosens the clothing and feels his pulse. Then Aaron recovers his breath and in a gasping voice speaks, while his friends listen in bewilderment.*]

AARON:
Are you still here? What has happened to me?

SWARTWOUT:
You've had too much excitement all day long!
I shall call the doctor. Bob will stay with you.
Do try relaxing, then you'll go to sleep.

AARON:
I hear loud thunder coming from the hold.
I see the quickly spreading flames burn up
The little merchant ship on which she sailed!
No rescuing vessels anywhere in sight!
No witnesses to see the holocaust,
Or hear the screams of dying passengers!
The howling winds add fury to the flames!
Everything at last has been consumed.
Charred wreckage floats upon the angry sea.
My child's dead body mingles with the rest,
The ship, the people, all have disappeared,
The same as though they never had been there!
Why is it that we call God merciful?
Why should I suffer in uncertainty?
Far better to have died long years ago
Than been in constant torment of despair!

[*Aaron's voice has been growing constantly weaker, and the last words are whispered through his dying lips. He drops the divorce papers, gives a faint gasp. His eyes protrude and limbs stiffen. He is dead!*]

SWARTWOUT [*Feeling Aaron's pulse and looking at Colonel Troup in despair*]:

196

Bob, he is dead! God be praised that we were here,
To be with him and witness this tragic scene!
His wife undoubtedly hastened his end!
No man has ever been so misunderstood
And so maligned by his contemporaries!
His life's ambition was to make his country
The greatest that the world has ever known!
That he should die in penury and disgrace
Is the irony of life's uncertain fate!

TROUP [*Putting his hand on the dead man's face and bending over him in grief*]:

We who knew him loved him and respected him.
It is now our duty and our privilege
To see that his desire is carried out
That his body should be placed at Princeton
Beside those of his father and grandfather.
When the truth's established, as it must be,
His name will shine in history with the great.

CURTAIN